Edited by
RICHARD POLENBERG
Cornell University

RADICALISM AND REFORM IN THE NEW DEAL

ADDISON-WESLEY PUBLISHING COMPANY
Reading, Massachusetts
Menlo Park, California · London · Don Mills, Ontario

This book is in the
ADDISON-WESLEY SERIES IN HISTORY

Robin W. Winks
Consulting Editor

 Printed in the United States of America. Published simultaneously in Canada. Library of Congress Catalog Card No. 72-171433.

For Lisa
Amy
Michael

CONTENTS

INTRODUCTION

The great depression that began in 1929 affected the reform movement in the United States in a variety of ways. In some respects it provided a relatively clear field for reformers, because it called into question the business ethos that had dominated the 1920's, produced a profound sense of national crisis, and submerged cultural issues of a divisive sort. Yet the depression also shaped the kind of reform that could take place and provided criteria by which its success would be gauged. The long years of economic adversity, therefore, created both opportunities and hazards for advocates of reform.

The coming of hard times caused many Americans to reject, temporarily at least, the creed of rugged individualism that had prevailed during the 1920's. So long as large numbers of people believed that "the business of America is business" and that Jesus Christ had been the prototype of the modern entrepreneur (had He not revealed every trait of the modern executive—patience, understanding and "amazing self-reliance"—asked Bruce Barton in *The Man Nobody Knows* [1925]) conditions were not congenial to reform. But businessmen who had once been eager to accept the credit for prosperity were obliged after 1929 to take the blame for the depression. That the crash dealt a hard blow to traditional assumptions regarding individualism, opportunity, and achievement was apparent in the eclipse of Herbert Hoover's reputation. In 1917 a letter addressed to "Miracle Man, Washington, D.C." found its way to Food Administrator Hoover; in 1932, it is safe to say, such a letter would not have been delivered to the White House.

The depression, by creating a sense of national emergency, afforded great scope to Franklin Roosevelt and the New Dealers. In years marked by foreclosure riots in the farm belt, hunger marches in the cities, and clashes between the army and unemployed veterans in the Capital, many Americans feared that the nation was edging perilously close to revolution and dictatorship. When Hoover asked for a ten percent cut in government salaries, for example, he secretly requested that Congress exempt the armed forces so that the troops would not be disgruntled if called upon to quell a rebellion. In retrospect it is clear that these fears were exaggerated, but many at the time gave them credence. The Midwestern congressman who told Roosevelt in 1933, "I will do anything you ask. You are my leader," expressed this sombre sense of crisis.

Cultural conflicts that had once divided reformers assumed less importance in the decade of depression. During the 1920's, rural followers of William Jennings Bryan and urban supporters of Alfred E. Smith shared many common objectives, but clashed over such issues as prohibition, immigration, and religious fundamentalism. These differences were overshadowed by the economic crisis. The restriction of immigration in 1924 had partially muted one of the main sources of disagreement; in the 1930's, with jobs growing scarcer by the day and with more people leaving than entering the country, virtually no one advocated lowering the bars. Prohibition, long a symbol of rural-urban conflict, was repealed in 1933; not only had it proven a failure, but wets could argue that legalizing liquor would create jobs and provide tax revenues. Franklin Roosevelt's skill in uniting rural and urban factions within the Democratic Party also helped heal cultural conflicts. While the coalition he created was in some ways unstable, for several years Roosevelt enjoyed the support of groups that formerly had been at odds.

Although the depression broke down many barriers to reform, it also imposed limitations upon the kind of reform that could take place. The New Deal centered almost exclusively on economic rather than political or moral reform. Even the political changes Roosevelt advocated, such as his attempt to enlarge the Supreme Court, were inspired by economic motives. Since New Deal programs were geared to recovery, they tended to satisfy those groups in society upon whom an upturn depended—business, agriculture, and labor. In its first two years, particularly, the New Deal epitomized "interest-group liberalism": it came to the rescue of organized and influential social groups but did little for those considered weak or marginal. Just as the depression ensured that reform would be economic in character, so it determined what the character of that reform would be.

The National Recovery Administration, the most important early New Deal measure to revive the economy, illustrated the broker state at work. Implicitly rejecting individualism and competition, it encouraged industry to draw up codes which regulated wages and prices, and in turn exempted industry from the antitrust laws. Planning, however, could have many meanings. For the most part those businessmen who preferred cooperation to cutthroat competition wished to make fundamental economic decisions themselves with a minimum of government interference. Many reformers, on the other hand, mistrusted business leadership. In their view all groups—labor, management, and consumers—should share in decision making, with the government acting as a balance wheel. Built into the

NRA, then, were disagreements about who should do the planning, how much of it there should be, and who should benefit. Eventually the NRA helped bring about a measure of recovery and eliminate such abuses as child labor in the Southern textile mills. But it often enabled large firms to consolidate control over the market. In those instances where big businessmen dominated the code-drafting process, they inserted provisions designed to keep production down and prices up. By 1935, even before the Supreme Court struck it down, the NRA had come under attack from consumers, labor, and small businessmen. The agency's initials, said the disenchanted, stood for "No Recovery Allowed."

New Deal agricultural policy also worked to the advantage of organized interest groups. The Agricultural Adjustment Administration accepted the domestic allotment plan, under which farmers received a subsidy for limiting production by reducing acreage. If the supply of foodstuffs could be held down by restricting output, the theory held, then prices would rise. Acreage reduction did in fact help restore farm income, which rose 50 percent from 1932 to 1936, but in most cases it was the wealthier farmer who benefited. Tenant farmers and sharecroppers, many of whom were Negroes, were injured when curtailing production deprived them of jobs or led to their eviction. Those tenants who remained received little in the form of cash benefits; all government checks went to the landlord, who frequently distributed payments unfairly, if he bothered to do so at all. There were officials in the AAA who tried to protect the landless farmers, but many of them were discharged in 1935. Since the crop reduction program could not succeed without the cooperation of the landlords, agricultural policy was tailored to their desires. Where the tenant was not driven from the land, his dependency upon the landlord was reinforced.

Between 1933 and 1935 the American labor movement made only slight gains. Widespread unemployment placed workers in a weak bargaining position, and company unions, which sprang up everywhere, also prevented independent organization. Leaders of the American Federation of Labor, who were unwilling to trespass on the jurisdictional rights of craft unions, opposed a mass organizing drive and justified their timidity by asserting that unskilled workers lacked the stamina, interest, or leverage to make good union members. Finally, the lack of government support retarded unionization. Although Section 7(a) of the NRA gave workers the right to organize, it neither provided machinery for choosing union representatives nor forced employers to bargain with their men. In

1934 President Roosevelt successfully opposed the efforts of Senator Robert F. Wagner to put teeth into collective bargaining statutes.

Caution also marked the policies of the Roosevelt administration with respect to the unemployed. Harry Hopkins, who headed the New Deal relief program, introduced important new concepts of public assistance. He thought that a sufficient amount for food, clothing, rent, and medical care should be supplied; that all in need should be eligible for aid; that payment should be in cash rather than grocery slips; and that work commensurate with an individual's skills should be provided. Despite these attempts to preserve the dignity of welfare recipients, early New Deal relief programs rested to a considerable extent on traditional assumptions. Officials in the Federal Emergency Relief Administration, for example, took for granted that states and localities would provide a substantial portion of relief funds, that an unbalanced budget was a source of danger, and that welfare, in the long run, eroded individual character.

By 1935 it was apparent that the attempt to reconcile the ambitions of major interest groups had not proven to be entirely successful. New Dealers who had reasoned that the depression resembled a war, and that all groups could therefore unite against a common foe, discovered that their analogy was misleading. Unlike a war, which brings prosperity and a relaxation of class rivalries, is directed against a foreign enemy, and is generally understood to require only a temporary sacrifice of liberties, the depression exacerbated class conflict, produced only an intangible opponent, and offered no assurance that liberties once surrendered would be restored. In large measure the early New Deal provided a test of the degree to which special interests could be subordinated to a more general interest; by 1935 it was clear that Franklin Roosevelt could not be "President of all the people."

Instead, his administration drew fire from both radicals and conservatives. Midway through Roosevelt's first term even many businessmen whose profits were higher than they had been under Hoover had come to detest the New Deal because it robbed them of status and prestige. Their most frequent complaint—that Roosevelt stirred up class hatreds—was often a way of saying that he did not show suitable deference to their own class. They insisted that business "confidence" would not return until the President scuttled his "radical" fiscal and labor policies, and they applauded every Supreme Court decision that went against the New Deal. Quite naturally, the President believed that conservatives misconstrued his purpose. "It is the same old story of the failure of those who have property to realize that I am the best friend the profit system ever had, even though I add my denunciation of unconscionable profits," he wrote.

Of course, many Americans claimed that the Roosevelt administration had done too little rather than too much. While some turned to socialism or communism, even more seemed to favor forms of radicalism that demanded less of a break with traditional values. Roosevelt's critics on the left who won the largest following promised that a radical improvement in one's fortunes could occur without a radical transformation of the social order. The Reverend Charles E. Coughlin, for example, supported a guaranteed annual wage but held that it could be attained without violating the sanctity of private property. Dr. Francis E. Townsend championed a scheme to provide $200 a month to retired persons over the age of 60; yet the plan, in his view, could be financed by a general sales tax and would not require deficit spending, heavy taxes on the wealthy, or an expanded federal bureaucracy. Similarly, Huey Long's "Share Our Wealth" movement seemed to point to a quick, easy, and sure road to good times.

Desertion on the right and pressure from the left combined to give the New Deal a more radical cast in 1935. In that year the administration won from Congress legislation that regulated holding companies in the field of electric power and imposed heavy taxes on corporation profits. This came close to representing a formal rejection of the NRA philosophy of business-government partnership. The administration also made tentative overtures to landless farmers by sponsoring the Resettlement Administration. Reversing his earlier position, Roosevelt lent support to the Wagner Act which, by enforcing collective bargaining, helped build the CIO and make possible the organizing drives of the late 1930's. Finally, 1935 witnessed passage of the Social Security Act and establishment of the Works Progress Administration, a relief program that went far beyond early New Deal welfare endeavors. Admittedly these programs usually represented compromises, often were inadequate, and occasionally, as in the case of the social security withholding tax, embodied regressive features. Yet, once legislation was on the books, discontent tended to be channeled into efforts to improve existing law rather than to alter the system.

After Roosevelt's mammoth victory in 1936 it seemed that he had forged an impregnable coalition and that four more years of reform would be on tap. But appearances were deceptive. Although Congress in 1937 and 1938 provided for construction of some low-cost housing, passed legislation to aid farm tenants, and enacted a wages and hours bill, these measures were badly watered down and represented only a fraction of Roosevelt's program to aid the needy. Just as the depression had in some respects determined the direction of reform, so it provided the standards by which the success of reform was judged. By 1937 the New Deal confronted the dilemma of any reform movement nurtured by depression: if the decline is halted, support for the movement evaporates; and if it is not, those in office must accept the responsibility for continued distress.

Obviously, Roosevelt's own proposals contributed to the waning of the New Deal, and nowhere was this more clearly revealed than in his attempt to enlarge the Supreme Court by adding up to six new members. The President wanted to reform the Court not only because it had wiped out certain New Deal measures, but also because it had adopted a line of constitutional reasoning that placed the Wagner Act and social security in jeopardy. Roosevelt chose one of the less radical courses available to him. Many critics suggested he should have endorsed a constitutional amendment, but these proposals—to limit judicial review by requiring a two-thirds majority for declaring an act unconstitutional, to give Congress authority to veto a Court decision, or to permit Congress to regulate the economy—were unrealistic and involved a more thoroughgoing alteration of political processes than did Roosevelt's plan. Moreover, if Roosevelt disparaged the age of the justices when he disagreed with their ideology, many of his critics attacked the plan less out of reverence for constitutional tradition than because they favored the Court's viewpoint. The President's plan was beaten in the end, but the Court reversed its position and approved the Wagner Act and other social legislation.

Court reform was one in a series of steps taken by the President during his second term to defend the New Deal. Just as judicial reform seemed necessary to protect social gains already on the books, so reorganization of government departments was required to create the administrative structure of the welfare state and to establish a permanent place for agencies performing new service functions. Roosevelt also believed that an extension of the liberal program required reform of the Democratic Party. Accordingly, the President proposed a broad-gauged plan of government reorganization, and in the Fall of 1938 attempted to defeat several conservative Democrats, most of them Southerners, who had blocked his program in Congress. But Roosevelt met with no more success in these endeavors than in the Court fight. Congress defeated executive reorganization in April, 1938, and most of those on the purge list won their primaries a few months later. Although it is unlikely that Roosevelt thought of judicial, administrative and political reform as part of a grand design, all were logically related to his efforts to preserve or expand the New Deal.

While his defeats in these battles cut into the President's base of support, they do not fully explain the weakening of the reform impulse. In a deeper sense the breakdown of the New Deal could be attributed to the effect of economic changes on popular attitudes. As William E. Leuchtenburg has pointed out, the very success of the New Deal proved to be its undoing: "The more prosperous the country became, the more people returned to the only values they knew, those associated with an individualistic, success-oriented society." Many people who were not doing well also looked upon reform with disfavor. The administration was severely censured for its inaction during the recession of 1937 and 1938. This slump, which resulted partially from Roosevelt's attempt to balance the budget by curbing outlays, dragged on for months before the administration brought forth a new spending program. Confronted by distress once again, many Americans turned against the party in power. In 1938 the Republicans won a sweeping victory, gaining 81 seats in the House, 8 in the Senate, and 13 new governorships.

Political considerations also figured in the fading of reform. During his first term Roosevelt had sought the backing of committee chairmen in Congress, many of whom had limited sympathy for reform but went along for personal or political reasons. Considering the nature of the emergency, Roosevelt probably had no alternative to that of working through the institutional structure of Congress, but the result was to bolster the strength of conservatives. In addition, the erosion of the New Deal after 1937 was related to a redefinition of its objectives. Reform was successful in Roosevelt's first term because it aided constituencies with a good deal of political influence; after 1937 the administration received less legislative support because it tried to help weaker groups. Finally, the New Deal may have sputtered to a halt because of the attention Roosevelt and his aides devoted to foreign affairs. Some domestic reforms apparently were shelved in order to gain congressional support for a policy of aiding Great Britain and her allies. By 1940, foreign policy and defense preparations had begun to absorb the energies of an increasing number of government officials.

Seldom do reform movements accomplish all that they promise, but they often clarify certain problems; the New Deal was no exception in either respect. During the 1930's, although the foundations of a modern welfare state were erected, unemployment did not end and prosperity was not restored. A sizeable number of New Dealers eventually endorsed the Keynesian approach to recovery, but Roosevelt was too much of a traditionalist to apply the formula of deficit spending in a consistent manner. As Howard Zinn has put it, "Many millions—businessmen, professionals, unionized workingmen, commercial farmers—had been given substantial help. Many millions more—sharecroppers, slum-dwellers, Negroes of North and South, the unemployed—still awaited a genuine 'new deal.' "

The New Deal did, however, raise questions central to an understanding of American political and economic development, and it is with these that the following essays are concerned. The articles in Part One explore some of the ways in which reformers viewed the relationship between special interests and the general interest: was it possible for government to act in behalf of the "general" interest; could this interest be defined apart from the ambitions of distinct groups in society; and could elected officials be trusted to act in accord with it? In Part Two, conservative critics of the Roosevelt administration consider some of the problems arising from the conflict between liberty and security: did the New Deal sacrifice personal freedom on the altar of security, or, by contrast, could liberty exist in a meaningful sense without economic security? The essays in Part Three illustrate some of the assumptions upon which radicalism rested during the depression. Was a radical alternative to the New Deal possible? If not, why not? And if so, what form might it have taken? The essays in the last section present conflicting appraisals of how well the New Deal succeeded in bringing about recovery and reform, and how well suited the American liberal tradition was to attaining these goals. While the character of American life has undergone a profound change since the 1930's and the specific issues confronting reformers and their critics have assumed new forms, the problems posed by the New Deal experience continue to be relevant.

PART ONE
THE REFORM IMPULSE

1
CHAOS OR CONTROL?
George Soule*

In the early 1930's American capitalism appeared bankrupt. Millions of jobless workers and their families were cold and hungry, not because the economy had produced too little but because it had produced too much. The spectacle of poverty in the midst of plenty led nearly all reformers to advocate some form of planning as an alternative to economic chaos, and to examine the two cases that seemed to offer historical precedents for constructive change: regulation of the American economy during the First World War and the Soviet Union's Five Year Plan. Few discussed the implications of planning more fully than George Soule, who had himself fought in the war and had later become an editor of the *New Republic.* In essays first published in 1932 and later incorporated into his book, *A Planned Society,* Soule reasoned that the cycle of boom and bust could not be eliminated without far-reaching changes in the economic structure. Yet precisely because he was aware of the institutional and ideological barriers to planning, Soule posed questions that were central to the reform position throughout the decade. To what extent did war and depression require planning, and did they require essentially the same sort of controls? How realistic was Soule's discussion of the similarities between the Russian and American systems? How much did his analogy clarify and how much did it obscure? Was it possible to ensure that a "National Economic Board" would be, as Soule wanted, "a representative of the

---

*Soule, George, Chaos or Control? *The New Republic* (March 23, 30, and April 6, 1932).

general interests?" Surely Soule went to the root of the matter when he conceded that "large objectives of planning must be defined and generally accepted"; but does he define these objectives in a tangible way? Was it likely that any such definition would in fact gain widespread approval? ☐

WE LEARN FROM WAR

To proposals that economic life be organized for collective purposes, it is customary for conservatives to answer that the task is beyond human capacity, or that, even if it could be done, it is something alien to the peculiar talents and values of America. These objectors forget that Americans, before the Russian Revolution, using their native wit and their domestic resources, once did a remarkable job of planning. Many of those who now advocate economic planning have been doing so, in one way or another, ever since the experiences of 1917-18, and mainly as result of the possibilities which those experiences suggested for better performance in times of peace.

This is a dangerous statement for anyone who believes in planning. It suggests to one with vivid memories of what happened during the War, that he wants such things as heatless Mondays, sugarless coffee, dollar-a-year men, useless wooden ships, Hog-Island confusion, an aircraft program which produces no airplanes, an artillery program which does not deliver a single gun in France, railroads accumulating a huge deficit and "under-maintained," big profits for meat packers, inflated wages, farmers held down to a minimum price for wheat and suffering from a broken promise about the price of pork, industries accumulating swollen surpluses.

There is no possibility of denying the fumbling, the mistakes, the occasional dishonesties, the annoyances, accompanying our industrial mobilization for war. But we cannot understand that experience without recognizing a number of striking facts.

We took about ten million men—or one-quarter of our gainfully occupied population—out of the production of goods and services useful in the ordinary life of peace. Some of these men were in the army, where they were engaged either in the destruction of life and property or in being trained for that destruction. The rest were occupied in equipping these men with the complicated and costly instruments of destruction, and all the other special material which they needed. Ten million of our ordinary productive forces not only had to be fed, clothed and housed as in peace, but themselves were engaged, directly or indirectly, in active destruction.

This immense dislocation was achieved within a few months; was carried out while the rest of the population was sustained on a level higher, on the average, than ever before.

The lesson of this experience cannot be escaped. By a deliberate collective effort, a tremendous expansion of our production was possible. By a deliberate effort, an amazing transfer of industrial energy from certain types of production to other types could be made in a short time. If that military and industrial army had been mobilized, not to kill, burn and shatter, but to substitute garden cities for slums, to restore soil fertility and reforest our waste regions, to carry out flood control, to increase the necessities of life available for those in the lower-income groups, we could have achieved in a short time a large number of really desirable objectives. It is nonsense to say that there is any physical impossibility of doing for peace purposes the sort of thing we actually did for war purposes. There may be obstructions in our institutions, habits and desires, but not in our equipment, skill and intelligence. This is not to say, of course, that we could do the peacetime job in precisely the same way.

What was involved in the economic organization for war?

Before the War, we had an economic society proceeding in the habitual, unplanned, competitive way. Goods were produced in response to the demand of purchasers. If the demand for a given product rose faster than the supply, its price increased; this stimulated production on account of the larger profits which could be made. Supply and demand were adjusted—so far as they were adjusted at all—through the price and profit mechanism. Nobody had much idea as to the total effect of what was going on. There was no inventory of resources, of capacity or of demand; no program laid out for the future, no control of prices or profits. The persons or groups who had purchasing power commanded the resources of production in their own interest.

Into this society, before the United States entered the War, there was inserted, like a force pump, an extraordinary demand for the materials desired by the Allied armies and nations. Governmental purchasing agents came over with enormous credits to buy large quantities of customary goods and also large quantities of special goods which we had not previously been making.

Then the United States entered the War. In addition to meeting the growing demands of the Allies, our industry and man-power had to fill the huge demands of our own governmental agencies. These agencies had all the money they wanted to spend. The government financed them to the limit. But they had almost no preparation for the job of raising and equipping a gigantic modern army. Not knowing exactly what they would need, they often ordered far more than they would need. They competed with one another for supplies which would not go around. They stepped on their own feet. Producers were pulled in every direction at once. Shortages developed everywhere—except in places where the need was not immediate. We had to make army cantonments, ships, tractors, tanks, guns, ammunition, clothing, and so on, to a total of thousands of items. And at the same time, men had to join the army. Something had to be done to subdue this planless waste. We had to arrange our demands on the one hand, and adjust the use of our resources to them on the other. This is what the economic war machinery was slowly designed for.

There was gradually developed an economic-planning system for the army, the navy and other great purchasers. These strove to work out a program in reasonable terms and to coördinate the various parts of it. Requirements were cleared daily through clearance committees in the War Industries Board, which would not allow orders to be placed unless the facilities for filling them were in sight. When it was necessary, on account of limited resources, to give priority to one type of demand over another type, a priorities committee in the Board decided which was to have the right of way. How far, for instance, should the available steel be allocated to ships, how far to guns, how far to railroad equipment? The most vital necessities of the War and the basic goods needed to sustain the civilian population were of course put first. Producing units, on the whole, accepted these priorities as a guide out of their confusion. When it was necessary to enforce priorities, the government did so through its control of railroad transportation or coal. It denied freight facilities or fuel to manufacturers who insisted on giving first place to goods not having priority status.

As a guide to clearance and priority, commodity sections in the War Industries Board kept constant tab on the capacities and existing production programs of the industries. They were in contact with committees representing the industries in question. Thus a rough production plan, not known by any one person at any particular time in its entirety, but worked out in countless details daily by many persons, was substituted for competitive demand and the planless adjustments of the price and profit system as the regulator of production. All this work was eventually headed up in the War Industries Board as the principal coördinator of war industries.

The Food Administration performed somewhat the same function for the food supply, coördinating the demands of the Allied governments and our own with those of the civilian populations arising through the ordinary channels of trade, matching demand against supply in the several kinds of foodstuffs, rationing where necessary, encouraging increase of output where necessary, working out essential substitutions.

The Fuel Administration took charge of the coal industry to see that it produced and shipped as efficiently as possible. It reduced many of the wastes of private enterprise, which often ships too much coal here and too little there, and ships it for greater distances than are necessary, in the competition for markets.

The Railroad Administration saw that the carrying capacity of all the railroads, considered as a national unit, was utilized to the best advantage. Rolling stock was pooled, and parceled out wherever necessary. Routes were changed to make them shorter and more economical. Terminals were unified. Instead of being run to the greater glory and profit of individual, competing companies, the railroads were run to provide as efficient as possible a national system of transportation.

The Shipping Board took charge of shipping with the same end in view. It mobilized the cargo space and the existing port facilities to fill the tremendous demand for ocean transportation as well as it could be filled. These activities, though less spectacular than the attempt to produce new ships through the Emergency Fleet Corporation, were fully as useful.

There was built up a system of federal employment exchanges to economize the supply of labor, and to direct it where it was most needed. A national machinery for the adjustment of wages, hours and conditions strove to deal with these matters rationally rather than allowing them to be decided on the basis of economic conflict alone. In order that the machinery might work, the right of labor to organize was, in many cases, implicitly recognized.

Price-fixing agencies, in the War Industries Board, the Food and Fuel Administrations and elsewhere, steered a course between two equally important objectives. One was to prevent such high prices for goods which were greatly in demand that the War would be unduly obstructed. The other was to set prices high enough so that industry, which was of course still operated on a profit-making basis, would be stimulated to the necessary productive effort. It was known that under war conditions great profits would be made, but the excess-profits tax was devised to convey some of these windfalls back to the government. As a device for social justice, the price-fixing and profit-limiting activity left much to be desired, but as a means of regulating production for war purposes it was moderately successful.

We entered the War in April, 1917; the Armistice was signed in November, 1918. While some of the preliminary steps were taken before our declaration of war, and the machine was not fully demobilized until 1919 and later, nevertheless this gigantic task of economic organization was performed mainly in the eighteen months of hostilities. Is there any wonder that there was a good deal of confusion in its operation? The marvel is that, by and large, it did the necessary job, that it saved us from a total breakdown.

What does the war experience teach us about the possibility of planning in peace? Is it true, as many have said, that we cannot organize our economic machinery for collective purposes unless we have to raise an army to fight an enemy?

One reason why it is supposed that we cannot do so is that, under the stress of war, the national government is permitted to do many things which would be constitutionally difficult in peacetime. The President, as Commander-in-Chief of the army and navy, has almost dictatorial powers. There is truth in this observation, and yet the economic organization of the War was by no means based upon mere political dictatorship. Little that was done had to be enforced by edict and threat of penalty. But there were other more important circumstances making possible wartime planning which do not ordinarily exist in peace. It will be useful to analyze these in order to see how, if at all, we can create substitutes for them when we are not at war.

The real compulsion, at bottom, was that furnished by the situation in which we found ourselves. Having decided to fight a war, to raise an army, to supply it and transport it, there were certain things which, we painfully discovered, had to be done to achieve that end. Understanding of these necessities brought compliance on the part of many persons which would not have been accorded to the exercise of arbitrary or capricious force. When an obstinate objection was met, the procedure followed was to explain the relevance of the proposed measures to the national purpose, and to ask the objector to face the responsibility of obstructing that purpose. This was the negative usefulness of a known and declared end.

Positively, it created in many an enthusiasm which made obstacles easier to overcome.

To supplement this means of bringing compliance there was the economic force furnished by the fact that so much purchasing power was concentrated in the hands of governments. A buying monopoly, whether it is public or private, is always in a position to dictate to sellers who are not subject to an equal degree of combination. If the government said, "Of the various things I am ordering, I want this first, that second and that third," the seller had good reason to agree. Likewise the government, as purchaser, was in a strong position to say, "You must supply me with essentials before you supply other, less important customers with nonessentials." These two types of economic dictation, which are practised in some degree in ordinary business life, become nothing less than the ability to enforce planning, when raised to a national scale. Of course the governmental purchasing power was in a favorable bargaining position with regard to price, as well as with regard to many minutiae of direction. The control that was exercised over industry was based, therefore, not primarily on constitutional political power, but on the economic power which naturally lies in the hand of a gigantic purchaser. No such concentration of purchasing power normally exists in peace.

The fact that governments were purchasing, and were purchasing to prosecute a war, likewise laid the reasoning basis for a plan. Because army and navy staffs were able to find out approximately what was needed, and the order in which it was needed, it became possible to draw up production schedules, to correlate them with one another, to rank the demands in an order of importance. There were objective criteria of judgment which could be used as the basis of decisions about production. These criteria were not easy to discover, and were not easy to apply, but they did exist. When our usual economic institutions are operating in peace, there is no single agency to specify and correlate demands.

Finally, there was a situation which is peculiarly important when we are considering planning as a method of avoiding depression and increasing the general standard of life. Depressions are characterized by a general lack of purchasing power; even in moderately prosperous periods there are usually idle plants and machinery which cannot be kept busy by the existing market demand. But, during the War, our industrial plant was operating at high pressure; there was almost no unemployment. Why did this happen? Merely because production was centrally adjusted? By no means. It was because governments were pouring a great stream of money into the markets. In times of peace there is almost never enough money seeking goods so that our productive plant works at full capacity. The sole exceptions are periods of speculative boom or inflation which shortly collapse into depression. That is one of the economic mysteries of an uncontrolled system. Perhaps the most important difference between the war economy and the peace economy was the presence in the former of abundant and insistent purchasing power. . . .

To sum up the lessons from our war planning, then, if we are to plan successfully for peace, we must establish the following four basic conditions:

1. We must have an objective which can arouse general loyalty and enthusiasm.
2. We must have an objective which is capable of being so concretely defined that it can decide questions as to how much we need to produce and in what order of importance the requirements are to be arranged.
3. We must have some means of mobilizing purchasing power—at least a substantial portion of it.
4. We must have some controlled means of increasing purchasing power. We must increase it enough but not too much, and we must distribute the increase in the right places.

RUSSIA'S ECONOMIC INVENTIONS

Soviet Russia has avidly made use of our machinery and engineering skill; can we make use of any of her economic inventions?

Two extreme groups of opinion deny that we can—the American Communists and the American reactionaries. The Communists call anybody who talks about planning without revolution a Fascist and an enemy of the working class; the reactionaries call anybody who talks about planning without revolution a Communist in disguise. If the argument is not thus to evaporate in the calling of names, we must look more closely at the facts.

The most obvious set of facts has to do with a difference in the general economic situation of the two nations. Soviet Russia began with a vast area touched only in spots with modern industrialism. Russia's economic difficulty was at first—and still is—a scarcity of goods, and of the means of producing goods, in relation to the ambition for a higher general standard of life.

The United States is much further along the scale of industrial development than Russia was at the time of her revolution. In our earlier years we had, like her, depended on our exportable surpluses in order to buy manufactures from abroad. We shipped out wheat, cotton, beef, pork and the like in exchange for machinery, cloth and fabricated articles of all kinds. We still have exportable surpluses of these things, as well as of oil, copper and many other natural products, though our timber and furs have been so ruthlessly exploited that they are no longer abundant. But now we have developed a great system of manufactures as well. We have exportable surpluses of automobiles, steel, machinery, cotton cloth and many other fabricated goods—or the equipment to produce such surpluses, which amounts to the same thing. Our economic problem is not that of scarcity, but, paradoxically, that of relative abundance. We have made so many goods that many of us are in danger of starving and freezing to death.

When the Soviet leaders became convinced that a world revolution was not imminent, they turned their attention to the rapid building of a great and rounded industrial plant within their own nation. The Soviet Union has increased its production at what is probably a more rapid rate than has ever been known before in any country. It has probably saved more capital in proportion to the national income than any other country has ever done. This statement sounds absurd in view of the fact that Russia has abolished "capitalism." But Russia has not abolished capital—the difference is that her saving and her capital are social instead of individual. All the national effort devoted to erecting factories and mills and hydro-electric plants instead of making more food and clothing was a process of saving and of capital formation just as truly as if each individual citizen had received in money a larger income and had saved about half of it for investment in factories, mills and hydro-electric plants.

If the United States were to develop a national economic plan, it would be compelled to seek quite different immediate objectives. We have no need of enduring great sacrifices in order to buy more things abroad, or to build up our basic industries. Physically, our job would be much easier than Russia's has been. We already have most of the material equipment which the Russian people have striven so heroically to acquire. But mentally, we should have a less simple and easy task than any she has faced so far. External necessities set the first goals for the Russian planners. It was not difficult for them to see what they had to attempt and why. In this respect their task was analogous to our war planning. They had to lay out a system of power plants, factories, mines and oil wells, acquire the materials and the skill to build them and train the people to operate them. This was a gigantic undertaking to execute. But, logically, its outlines were pretty clear. There were definite criteria of judgment as to what was needed, and where, and how much, and when, just as there were in our economic war machine. Purchasing power was largely mobilized by the government itself, especially since the monopolized foreign trade played so large a part in the scheme. But the United States could not begin its planning with a governmental attempt to build a brand-new industrial plant. We could not create employment in quite that way. Slavish imitation of the first Soviet Five Year Plan would get us nowhere. It is irrelevant to our situation.

There are, however, other elements in which the Russian economy is more like our own than either the propagandist advocates or the opponents of the Soviets are willing to admit. Let us list briefly a number of these broad points of similarity:

1. *Financial institutions.* It uses money; it has banks; it even resorts to borrowing by the government and the payment of interest.
2. *Profits.* Profits are made by its industrial and commercial units—though these profits are not distributed to private owners.
3. *Capital.* Capital is accumulated and is invested in new productive equipment.
4. *Unequal rewards.* The payment for work is unequal (though the inequalities are not nearly so great as in this country). Piece rates are widely used in the payment of wages.
5. *Accounting.* Careful accounts are kept in each factory, store or other unit, and the management of each is responsible for operating it without a deficit on the books.
6. *Free choice by consumers.* Individual purchasers buy, with money, the goods that are for sale in cooperative and other stores. They exercise free choice in what they buy, so far as they can do so within the range of articles offered for sale and the prices charged. Rationing is resorted to only in the case of necessities of which there is a scarcity, and then only so long as a scarcity exists.
7. *Decentralized management.* The details of industrial and commercial life are not directed by a central board or a bureaucracy. Given a central decision on main policies, as much stress is laid on decentralization of activity and responsibility as in most large American corporations.

8. *Change and adjustment.* Industrial life is not governed by a hard-and-fast plan which is not subject to change. Changes in planning are constantly made. Mistakes occur, are acknowledged and corrected. Soviet economy has probably changed and developed more rapidly than any other in history. The planning function is not primarily a restricting one, but a stimulating one.

But here we verge into the differences between the Soviet economic system and our own. The similarities have been emphasized in order to show that a planned economy—even so thoroughly planned an economy as the Russian—does not involve so drastic a change in all our habits and ways of behaving as it may appear without careful study of the facts.

Having observed general similarities between the Russian system of management and our own, it remains to point out the differences.

The central difference is that in the Soviet Union there are basic decisions as to the policy and objectives of the collective life, whereas in our society the necessity for making such decisions is not acknowledged and there is nobody charged with making them. These decisions are made, in Russia, by the Communist party. The policy decisions are made by political instrumentalities, and political activity is dominated by a political machine. It is, to be sure, a political machine with high social standards, which rigorously checks graft and personal ambition. But it is important to note that central to the whole endeavor is political control of a recognizable type. The difference is that in Russia this control is devoted single-heartedly to the hammering out of collective policies, whereas our political control serves, in the main, the ends of the varied private interests which pay its bills. This circumstance is one of the things which prevents our political machines from attending more than they do to general policies. The assumption in this country is, whenever any assumption is made, that the interaction of all the numerous private interests will automatically produce the most desirable general policy. We abandoned that assumption temporarily for war purposes, and we must abandon it whenever we want to tackle national economic planning.

The basic decisions made by the Communist party include such things as that the State shall own and control land and natural resources, factories, machinery, banks, stores, merchandising agencies, etc., and that all these things shall be used for the benefit of the whole population (except of those whom the socialist State regards as enemies or useless persons, like saboteurs, priests, private traders and private employers).

It does not follow that exactly the same basic decisions would have to be made by a policy body in the United States or another country. Public opinion in the world has been so conditioned by industrialism and the liberal democratic slogans which accompanied its birth that the main objective of an acceptable policy in any country would almost necessarily be the same as the Russian objective–enhancement of the general popular well being. There might, however, be more doubt as to whether it was necessary, in pursuit of this end, for the State to expropriate all productive or business property. It is perfectly possible to conceive of a policy-making body deciding to experiment with other means of control before concluding that general state ownership was necessary. It may be that private productive property is not in itself incompatible with the general welfare, but is incompatible only to the extent that it prevents or resists planning exercised in behalf of the workers by hand and brain. Experiment might be made to determine how stubborn and unavoidable that resistance would be. . . .

In planning for war, the United States was successful largely because the government had mobilized a large amount of purchasing power. In Russia, though political dictatorship plays a large part, the mobilization of purchasing power is obviously important as an economic instrument of carrying on the daily life of planning. Individual consumers' purchasing power is mobilized through the coöperatives, which are thus enabled to present a schedule of consumption to productive industry. The government, by its control of credit and capital investment, mobilizes the purchasing power of the several industries for raw materials, for one another's products and for imports.

Likewise, Soviet Russia has a means of increasing purchasing power as her production increases. She can distribute it in wages, or collect it in profits to be paid out again for more production, as she pleases. It is difficult to see how any crisis could possibly arise from such a thing as general "over-production" in the Soviet economy, if it can be operated in practice as in theory it is laid out.

And Russia has an objective which is capable both of arousing general enthusiasm and of furnishing bases of judgment for its planning decisions.

These are the outstanding lessons to be learned, so far, from Russian planning. There is here no attempt to approve or disapprove, to predict success or failure, even to follow more than the main outlines of what is, in fact, a highly complex and rapidly changing system. But, from a cool distance which permits a large perspective, it would appear that we can perhaps make better use of the Russian experience than many have thought. Though in many respects the Soviet system differs widely from our own, the economic and engineering techniques which it is using are not wholly foreign to thought and practice in North America.

A CHALLENGE TO INACTION

It would be futile to lay out "a plan" for a society in the same way that an architect can make a set of drawings and specifications for a building, in which all details of measurement, of stress and strain, of material, are set down in advance and have but to be followed in detail. Social-economic planning is not a hard-and-fast, completely predetermined scheme. It is a method, a technique, a way of attacking problems. It develops in practice. It must be learned, and like other disciplines of education, it can be learned only by doing.

Least of all could any individual write a valid national plan. Successful planning is not only a method, it is a social process, in which whole communities must participate. They must have the will to coöperate for common ends. Large objectives of planning must be defined and generally accepted. These must be translated into more detailed goals and standards for action day by day, not by one man, or even by a central board only, but with the aid of agencies which ramify throughout society, from the largest unit to the smallest. Only when we have the will to plan, can the necessary goals be chosen and the necessary machinery be set up. And only when we have done that, can we proceed to learn national planning in the way in which it must be learned–by experiment, by successes and failures, by continual modification and development. Even our objectives are likely to be changed in this process. The final result cannot be foreseen clearly from the beginning. All we can do is to recognize the need for a beginning, and to outline in a large way how that beginning may be made. . . .

There must be a central administrative organ of some sort for each important industry–and by industry in this connection is meant not merely "productive" industries like steel and automobile manufacture, but transportation, retail distribution, banking. Single industries must be got under control if we are to do things like establishing rising wage standards without increasing prices, relating production and new investment to estimated demands for consumption. And each of these central administration organs must have its planning agency, its statistical staff. . . .

There is needed a National Economic Board at the top, representing the whole public. This would correlate the plans and practices of the various industries with one another. It would bring together the relevant statistical material from all sources and fill in the gaps. It would work out a general plan for raising the lowest incomes and regulating the flow of investment and credit. It would turn its attention, like a searchlight, on these areas and industries which were causing trouble and obstructing the general program. It would advise government as to its responsibilities in the carrying out of the program.

This Board should be composed, not of bargaining representatives of various interests, but of qualified experts representing the nation as a whole. It should, of course, have an adequate staff of economists, statisticians, engineers and accountants. As a representative of the general interest, it ought to be established by law, with certain duties and powers. It should be supported by governmental appropriation, and appointed by the President, with the advice and consent of the Senate.

One of the first duties of a Board like this would be to help in working out the best form of organization for each industry, and represent the public in the drafting of that organization. It would, for instance, call together representatives of the soft-coal mine owners, the consumers of coal, the coal technicians and the organizations of labor in coal. It would say to them: "Your industry is, and has been for years, one of the chief obstacles to a genuine prosperity for the nation. It must be organized to pay higher wages without charging unduly high prices, give steady employment, and offer efficient service. What needs to be done to control your industry and make it a sound unit in a national economy? We are instructed by Congress to aid you and your experts in formulating a plan of organization for these purposes. We are delegating our own experts to advise you at every stage of your researches and deliberations. We will give you two years to produce a proposal, though we should like one as soon as possible. When your proposal is ready, we will either approve it or disapprove it, having in mind the objectives to be sought. If you do not produce a plan or do not produce one which we can approve, we are instructed by Congress to make one of our own. If legislation is required, we shall recommend to Congress the measures we approve. After the coal organization is set up, we shall continue to keep in close touch with it, in order to see that the objectives are approached, and in order to correlate your annual plans for wages, employment, production, prices, profits and investment with those of other industries."

In tackling an organizing job of this kind, the Board would have in mind the possibility, not merely of a trade association or cartel, but of large consolidations under some form of public regulation, and of complete public ownership by such a device as a publicly owned corporation which would buy out the existing individual owners with debentures. The Board should not be limited in its ultimate choice by any bias in favor of "private enterprise." It should choose the form which, after thorough examination, seemed best suited to the ends in view. My own opinion is that in this case, public ownership would be found most desirable, as in other basic industries.

The Board would, in the same manner, put up to the construction industry and its chief customers the task of organizing to prevent the wide swings of activity which now do much to shove us to heights of inflation and then plunge us down again. It would put experts to work in order to see what would have to be done to provide good housing, in healthful and pleasant surroundings, for the majority of the population which now cannot afford it. This is one of the greatest unused opportunities to provide a better standard of life and, at the same time, furnish a large amount of employment in the building industry and those which supply its materials. It is a magnificent way to use surplus savings, instead of pouring them into unneeded and unused equipment.

So the problems of each productive industry would be approached, industry by industry.

Control of the banking system would have to be strengthened. And we should have to plan new investment, to plan the use of credit.

Distribution would be an important field for organization. The Board would have to get the chain stores, the department stores, the mail-order houses, to combine on a plan for reducing distributive waste, for better standardization and specification of goods in the interest of their usefulness to the consumer. There would be needed, also, a means of estimating future requirements of consumption, area by area. This would be an extension and completion of market studies already in existence.

There would have to be, under the Board, a labor administration. It would oversee a nationwide system of employment exchanges to bring workers and jobs together, and currently provide the facts concerning unemployment and labor shortages. It would have a training department to prepare for employment elsewhere any group of workers who had to be transferred from an obsolescent industry or one in which mechanization was so rapid that full employment could not be furnished by expanding demand. It would administer unemployment insurance to tide over unavoidable periods of joblessness. This would, in itself, provide a stabilizing influence by maintaining the purchasing power of the unemployed. It would keep close tab on wages and hours, so that the Board would know whether its general wage policy was being carried out. The labor administration would of course work closely with the labor organizations. The growth of these should be encouraged: legal restrictions on their expansion should be removed.

Under a well planned system, there ought to be no grave problem of "technological unemployment." Everyone can be kept busy for normal working hours providing the goods and services needed to bring the mass of the population up to a moderately enjoyable standard of living if only we can find the means of sufficiently enlarging purchasing power. If technical advances go so far that we really produce more than people want, no matter what their capacity to pay, shorter working hours can be substituted for larger production. Every time work is made easier, we can enjoy the result in more product or more leisure, as we choose.

Various regional-planning agencies are necessary, to lay out our facilities properly on their geographical base, to furnish the proper setting for, to correlating our houses, factories, roads, water supplies, forest and farm areas, recreation regions, railroads, power lines. Thus the work would be decentralized geographically as well as industrially. The beginnings of such bodies are already in existence in several states and regions.

This is an attempt to apply a scientific, experimental method to the solution of the question concerning how much compulsion it is necessary to exercise over business in effectuating national planning. It does not make the decision wholesale, and in advance of investigation and trial.

The planning activity here sketched would, if it succeeded, fulfill the requirements learned from our war experience with planning. It begins with an objective capable of arousing enthusiasm—a war against poverty, unemployment, insecurity, an expansion of the standard of living, a great national effort toward a finer civilization, a desire to do a good job and use properly the tools we have. By its devices to increase purchasing power and predict consumer demand, and its control of expenditures for new investment, it builds up the economic equivalent for political police power. It can decide questions as to how much we need to produce and in what order. It can point out to industry the necessities inherent in the situation—the facts which, in the end, exert authority. For the very essence of planning is not just someone's capricious desire to plan, but organized, democratic adjustment to the situation created by modern technology. The practical problem is to develop out of this situation the will to plan collectively, and to give that will a sufficiently powerful political implement so that the effort to plan may be begun, and carried through.

2
PRIVATE BUSINESS AND PUBLIC OPINION
Adolf A. Berle*

In the 1932 campaign Franklin Roosevelt summoned the services of the "brains trust," a group composed primarily of Columbia University professors. Included were Rexford G. Tugwell, Raymond Moley, and Adolf A. Berle. The youngest of the three was Berle who had entered Harvard at the age of fourteen, been graduated at seventeen, and taken his law degree at twenty-one. After a year's apprenticeship as clerk for Louis D. Brandeis and infantry service during the war, Berle took up the practice of corporate law in New York City. Then, in 1927, he accepted a professorship at Columbia. His most influential book, *The Modern Corporation and Private Property* (1932), was written in collaboration with Gardiner C. Means. Berle and Means argued that the growing divergence between ownership and management in the modern corporation—as compared with the classical model in which both functions were united in the person of a capitalist—had upset most traditional assumptions about economic behavior. They also maintained that the growth of the corporation had "brought a concentration of economic power which can compete on equal terms with the modern state." Berle's concern with the relationship between private business and state power was nowhere more clearly illustrated than in this article which he wrote nine months after Roosevelt took office. Starting with the premise that the New Deal had established new ground rules under which business was to operate and that the issue was no longer whether but *how* the state would protect its citizens from economic adversity, Berle went on to consider some of the problems presented by government regulation. While he conceded that purposeful minorities might seek to exploit government for selfish purposes, Berle thought that the danger could be averted by adopting a pragmatic approach which shunned "predetermined sweeping solutions."☐

---

*Berle, Adolf A., Private Business and Public Opinion, *Scribner's,* XCV (February, 1934), 81-88. Reprinted by permission of Mrs. Beatrice Bishop Berle.

As the first year of the new administration draws to its close, the clash of philosophy in American politics becomes increasingly clear. This is natural enough. The administration was born in a period of extreme emergency; and in emergencies all hands move to support the government from combined motives of patriotism and self-defense. Only after the immediate danger is got out of the way does debate recommence. Out of that debate the lines of policy emerge. In our political system it is of greatest importance, first, that there be debate, and, second, that the debate have an issue. An undiscussed policy is apt not to take into consideration important elements of national opinion. Discussion without policy leads merely to confusion. This debate is now in progress, and it is perhaps worth while to indicate the underlying forces which are governing it.

As I see them, these forces lie very deep. On the one side there is a very real belief that the orthodox or classic economics affords the principal basis for organizing the world. Among the classic premises are that the world is best served by a free exchange of goods, hence that tariffs should come down and that foreign trade should find its natural levels. Further, that the free operation of business will find its balance, hence that as little restriction should be put on business as can be. Further, that when trade decreases, and with it employment, the proper solution is to increase trade by lowering prices, and accept, as a necessary concomitant, lowered wages. And so on down the line.

What the orthodox economic view (which is, in substance, the conservative view) has not been able to cope with is the human revolt against the sacrifices imposed on individuals by this system. Let us leave aside the question whether the revolt is intellectually justifiable, and deal realistically. There is not free trade; popular pressure in every part of the world has forced subsidies or tariffs or what not. There is not freedom of price in great areas of commerce; monopolies, interest charges, regulated rates, and the like, have prevented this. There is not acceptance of the doctrine that wages may be reduced to whatever world level the situation affords, as a means of increasing the sale of goods. Laborers resist the process. Taking practically every premise of orthodox economics, you will find that there has been a rebellion of popular opinion against the results of orthodox economics, sufficiently strong to force policies on nations throughout the world, which make acceptance of that philosophy a little unreal.

Governments rarely initiate philosophies. They accept philosophies which have been worked out by intellectuals, carried forward by teachers, churches, clubs, newspapers, makers of public opinion; and they interpret these philosophies, not in pursuing a predetermined plan of campaign, but in meeting individual situations as they arise. The philosophy is often vague; it crystallizes only when a problem has to be met.

In countries like England and America, this method of handling affairs is historic. It is possible for a Russian Revolutionist or an Italian Fascist to make up in advance a philosophy, crystallize it into a plan, and announce, through the medium of virtual dictatorship, that this is the plan which will be carried out unless an international catastrophe engulfs the country, or a revolt engulfs the government. The Anglo-Saxon and the American systems tend to discard predetermined sweeping solutions. But their statesmen have views, and these views determine the extent to which the government is prepared to go in meeting any given emergency. Like other men, statesmen have minds, and their thought grows as they work. Like other men, their minds have limits; there are adventures they will accept, and adventures they will decline. The real limit of governmental action is determined by the line at which a responsible statesman will refuse to undertake responsibility, when he has the unquestioned backing of his people, and by the limit which public opinion, working through political channels, imposes on him.

In this light, an examination of Federal policy in the United States today becomes extremely interesting.

I

The great contribution which Mr. Roosevelt's "New Deal" has made in American politics has been a tremendous expansion of the area in which his government is prepared to accept responsibility.

Prior to this time the conditions under which business would function were regarded as (in substance) exclusively a matter for the determination of business men. If business declined to function, asserting that conditions made it impossible to do so, the job of the government was to create conditions under which it could or would work, and having done so, to let business resume its usual course. This is possible when the human revolt mentioned above is not of serious proportions. But if, humanly, the mass of people in a country is unwilling to accept life under conditions which seem necessary to private business men, an impasse is created. In terms of practical politics, the congressman, the senator, the executive, the administrative official, each is faced with overwhelming pressure from the people who put him into his position, to lay down a set of ground rules. Business, on the other hand, declines to accept these ground rules, and commerce stops. You can tell almost automatically what the temper of a political movement is, from the popular reaction to this kind of impasse. If the business structure on the whole satisfies the general desire of the great mass of the population, the pressure will shift; instead of desiring different ground rules—wanting to change the rules of the game—the pressure at once becomes a demand that the rules of the game be adapted to the desires of business men, of merchants, of bankers, so that the machine can once more start moving. But if (and this seems to be the case now) the general desire is to insist on certain conditions of life, and to treat as public enemies men who decline to accept these rules, or who do not wish to function in business or banking or trade under them, then it is plain that social force is requiring a fundamental structural change, and the government must either meet the situation or abdicate in favor of a group which can.

The Roosevelt administration faced exactly this situation in the bank holiday. As matters then stood, the public did not have sufficient confidence in banks to continue using them, and their functions temporarily stopped. Faced with a national emergency, there was practically unanimous support for Mr. Roosevelt's government when it first declared a national bank holiday, which involved assumption by the national government of responsibility for the entire banking system; next, when it changed the banking laws, granting to the government almost unlimited powers in aid of the banks; and third, when it permitted an almost indefinite extension of the functions of the Reconstruction Finance Corporation and similar organizations in credit matters. Banking having failed to function, the government was given wide powers both to assist banking, to control it, and, within limits, to assume banking functions on its own behalf.

This, of course, resulted from the combination of a variety of circumstances. It did not present the cleancut issue which we may have later. There was no great demand in 1931 and 1932 for a change in the general rules of banking. There was a distinct feeling that many bankers had abused their position, and a belief that, by reason of that fact, and of other accompanying facts, banks were unsafe. But this rapidly developed . . . into a feeling that the system itself left something to be desired. A very large number of bankers, among them the most reputable members of the profession, joined in that feeling.

In industry an almost exactly similar phenomenon took place. Those who were familiar with the situation immediately after the bank holiday recall the piling up of pressure from all quarters, which led to the passage of the National Industrial Recovery Act. Labor considered that it could not maintain its wages, and that it did not propose, through wholesale wage cut, to go back to a sub-subsistence standard of living. Business men found themselves unable to make money, and were prepared to subscribe to the theory that higher wages throughout the country and increased distribution of the industrial income would be better for business. All of them agreed that to leave industry unorganized would continue an impossible situation to a point of general break-down. In an endeavor to meet all these points of view, the National Recovery Administration took form. This involved an adventure in industrial organization as yet unknown to the American system; but the mere logic of government required it. . . .

II

We have come, then, to the new force which appears in government today. We happen to see it in America, but the same force is awake throughout all of western civilization. Whereas before there was no alternative to private business, today there is always an alternative, and the alternative may come into play at any moment. A government which did not directly participate in the economic life of the country—that is, which did not directly engage in business—was necessarily forced to create conditions under which private business could operate. A government prepared to do the job itself, however, has far wider latitude in determining policy. It can enter the arena only if its people support it in so doing; it will be supported only if its people decline to accept conditions which private business feels essential. Within limits, of course, a government can crystallize sentiment in its own country, in favor either of private or of public business. But it can do so only in the light of prevailing conditions. When private business is doing the job acceptably and honestly and well, a government which undertook to whip up enthusiasm for, let us say, entering the steel business, or taking over the railroads, would be met either with hearty laughter, or with prompt repudiation at the polls. Where business is not functioning acceptably, the popular demonstration is in exactly the opposite direction.

Rarely does a government go out and undertake to invade a territory occupied by private business, unless private business has itself created a situation believed to be intolerable; or, perhaps through no fault of its own, has reached a point where it cannot carry on. No sane statesman wants to take on the work, the responsibility, the disappointments, the difficulties and the incalculable complexities of any large-scale private business, if he can keep a country on an even keel without doing so. Equally, when the business is necessary to the national economy, he can hardly avoid tackling the job, if private functioning has ceased. In a word, governments today have a mandate to see that their economics continues to operate. Included in that mandate is a grant of power adequate to perform that function. This is true, whether the incumbent is Grau San Martin in Cuba, or Mr. Hoover or Mr. Roosevelt in the United States. Even Mr. Hoover, you will recollect, when the investment-banking machinery and the banks failed to function in connection with existing laws, formed the Reconstruction Finance Corporation, and made the first great entry of the United States Government into what had been private business. He did this, not because he wanted to, but because he had to; and the pressure came far more from Wall Street than it did from the country, though the country promptly and unanimously supported the move.

It is after one of these situations has arisen, and after the territory has been occupied, that the economic and social philosophy of a government really begins to appear. The whole difference between Mr. Hoover and Mr. Roosevelt lay in the fact that Mr. Hoover considered his occupation of the territory as temporary, as bridging over a gap which the business men found themselves unable to over-pass, and in aid of the business men, who were carrying on the functions. Mr. Roosevelt's government conceives that, having taken over the function, it also has taken over the responsibility for the results. These results are measured in terms of the effect on the life of the community. The Reconstruction Finance Corporation, for example, in Mr. Hoover's time was a substitute for a private bank, and existed to assist private banks and bankers. In Mr. Roosevelt's administration, it was conceived that with that assistance went the right to insist that the banks should produce certain general effects. Specifically, they ought to make available enough credit for the community; and they ought not to be merely strategic centres from which individuals could dominate the interests which necessarily flow through the banks.

It is at this point that social philosophy really (and literally) becomes serious business.

A government which has taken over responsibility for a great business function can consider the situation in terms other than those of strictly private business. Let us assume, for example, that the city of New York takes over the transit lines. A five-cent fare, let us suppose (though it is not demonstrated), will not pay the cost of the service. A private business man in that situation must either raise his fare, or lower his wages, or go into bankruptcy and cut down his interest charge, or go out of business. A government, however, may look the situation squarely in the face and may determine that it would be preferable to run the transit lines at a slight loss, socialize that loss and cover it by means of taxation, in the general interests of life in the city of New York. The debate then shifts from the problem of the essential price in private hands to a question of social philosophy in municipal hands. A municipality can (as private owners cannot) resolve the controversy in the sense that it is better for the city and for its inhabitants to have cheap transit, and to require certain groups, through taxes, to pay the loss, on the ground that they profit by the cheap service. Illustrations of this kind might be multiplied almost indefinitely.

Enough has been said, I think, to indicate why discussions as to government in business, redistribution of wealth, the chance for all individuals to live their lives, the (approximate) equality of opportunity and the like, have ceased to become academic debates. With the government, which is to say the entire organized force of the people and of the community, taking a part in the performance, willing and able if necessary to assume the stellar rôle, the part of social philosophy moves up from that of an intellectual aside to that of a Greek goddess which can appear from the machine at any time.

III

For myself, I have whole-heartedly welcomed the great gate which has been opened in America by the New Deal. For the first time in my generation it becomes possible to think broadly, and the instruments for making the kind of country one would like to have become approximately available. In spite of an intellectual predilection for orthodox economics, I have to recognize that orthodox economics, unfortunately, are not to be found anywhere in any world available for me to live in. For the time, at least, they are a dream only. Realistically, I have to live in a world in which men insist on making economics, rather than economics making men; and if that is the situation under which I have to work, I have no choice but to prefer a government which takes into its hands all necessary tools with which to work. I have a bias in favor of the freedom of private business; and a still stronger bias in favor of the general idea that business men can solve problems both in social philosophy and in economic functioning, if they are willing to regard themselves as a public service of supply, and not as a private racket. But as an honest student of finance, I have to admit that private finance and private business, under the conditions prevailing today, may break down at any time. This is partly due to their own fault, and that can be rectified by education and by change of personnel. It is partly due to the fact that in certain respects, notably those revolving around large corporations and the financial and banking systems, the structure is radically wrong. And, like every sane person, I cannot allow my emotions to get away with my judgment; I cannot say that, because on the whole I like the individualism of private property and of private business, therefore I will nail my flag to the mast, although my family, my friends, and the population generally starve, in the vindication of a noble theory. Nostalgia is never a substitute for realism.

And yet it must be recognized that there are tremendous dangers involved in the new orientation of government and business. Before placing these, it is perhaps well to lay down the lines of the discussion as it now stands.

There is as yet no veto on private profit. The profit motive, essential in a developing country, has still a tremendous place in any economic civilization. For example, it must continue to function in developing new inventions; in pushing out the frontiers, either geographically or scientifically; in devising new forms of organization. It is not easy to think of a civilization which is not constantly pushing out its frontiers in terms of goods and of services, though geography is beginning to be a restricted field.

But there are claims of the community which are regarded as superior to private profit, and there are great areas of profit which are no longer considered legitimate, because they impose sacrifices on the community. The illegitimate profits may be defined as those in which a business transaction results in a profit to an individual at a greater expense to the community at large. For instance, in my factory I may install a machine, for, say, $10,000, which will do the work of, say, 200 men. This saves me money, and my profits increase. The 200 men are thrown out of work; it takes them, let us say, two years to learn a new trade or to find new jobs; and the aggregate of their losses is greater than my profit. This is not a real profit—only an illusory one. What I win, some one else has paid—the men themselves, if they have savings; the community, if they go on a relief line. Again, an illegitimate profit is obtained where the individual business man makes his money not because he has rendered a service to the community, but because through strategic position he has levied toll upon one group or another. For instance, he may be able unduly to depress his wages, and get his profit at the expense of the community standard of living; or by reorganizing a railroad he may be able to take a rakeoff. In other instances, profits become simply too expensive for the community to pay. You might run a City Hospital Department at a profit by charging every one who applied for medical assistance a fee commensurate with the cost; but public health is more necessary than private profit in that field of human endeavor, and the profit system is rightly scrapped, in favor of a socialization of losses.

You may almost test the social philosophy of a government by areas in which private profit is considered essential, and those in which community service is considered more important. Practically every function which a modern government now performs was at one time regarded as private business. The collection of taxes was for centuries a private enterprise, and the job was "farmed out" to one or another group, who made fortunes at it. Roads, post-offices, public health, sanitation, schools, hospitals, all started as private enterprises. They were gradually absorbed into the community or socialized system, either directly, as governments took them over, or indirectly, as they were folded into a system of private charity and relief. The advance of modern civilization can almost be measured by the rising demands which a community as a whole makes on the area of private activity.

The first danger, and a very real one, is that a government, entering a new area, will over-measure the claims which a community makes, mistaking the insistence of particular groups in their own interest for a demand which the community is entitled to make in the name of all. This danger arises partly because organized minorities will always exert more pressure than unorganized majorities, and still more through the thoroughly vicious practices of lobbies, who also frequently have machinery for publicity at their disposal. A really high-powered lobby will ask for something which its group has no business to have, and be fully prepared to make a devastating personal attack on any one who stands in the way. The public official, particularly if he is honest, does not have access to equivalent publicity in answer, and the more honorable he is, the less he enjoys putting his reputation at that kind of hazard.

One of the problems we shall undoubtedly have to struggle with is that of the massing of groups of interests and employees who have come intermediately under government regulation or directly into the sphere of government action, and who endeavor accordingly to establish a claim on the community in their own behalf. Against this it must be pointed out, however, that the losses occasioned by this process are not net. A private business in a strategic position will take the same amount of money away from the community, not through a process of political pressure, but through its commercial activities; and the result will be concentration of wealth in the hands of the owners or managers of the business. These amounts are less than a really first-class raid on the community treasury by a minority; but they are not dispersed, and therefore contribute less to economic life as a whole. Further, as more and more groups come into play, they tend to balance each other out. I should question whether, proportionately, any group could equal the record of the Civil War veterans or the World War veterans today. Those groups were almost alone in the field, in their halcyon days; today they have to compete with many other groups, which realize that if any one group overdoes it, all must suffer in the end.

Another danger—and this perhaps the greatest—is that human nature does not change, merely because government has entered the field of economics. The racketeer in business is the grafter in politics; the unrestrained exploiter in finance is the ambitious demagogue in government; the irresponsible and cut-throat competitor in commerce is the intriguer and self-aggrandizer in a government job. There is, however, a distinct difference in point of view. For one thing, the holder of a strategic commercial position who is abusing it can be dislodged only by a terrific outbreak of popular sentiment, whereas a single general election can explode the position of an unscrupulous or unworthy public servant. For another, the objective in business is precisely this aggrandizing and accumulative process; whereas in public service, that very fact alone makes an individual the object of suspicion. Briefly, the ideal and object of the whole game is shifted.

The last and most discussed danger has been that individual initiative is reduced as the area of government entrance into economic function increases. For myself, I have never been able to feel too much discouraged on this score, though there is something to be said for it. Private initiative, when used in that argument, almost invariably relates to the money-making initiative. And yet, private initiative can be translated into so many other fields! There is no restraint, for example, upon initiative in art, in literature, in finance, in study, in the whole field of the humanities. Perhaps a little less private initiative in the field of making money would not be such a bad thing, after all. We probably shall not get to the stage of having, as Plato once hoped, kings who are philosophers, or philosophers for kings; but we might make some progress toward a stage in which a man was esteemed in the community, not because he had manipulated himself into a great commercial position, but because he was making a steady contribution to the thought, the art, or the operation of civilization as a whole. In fact, we are making progress along that line now. Included among the men who are emerging now is a much larger percentage of those who attained their position because they thought deeply, and contributed honestly to the general welfare. If this is one of the by-products of the New Deal, surely there will be little cause for complaint, and we shall be less at a disadvantage when our European friends assert that our outlook has been entirely too material.

Finally, we may take comfort in the knowledge that mankind is continually achieving the impossible. That is, after all, the saving grace of being men. Like Prometheus, we always do assault the heavens, and bring back the impossible fire. This is as true of organized government and economics as it is true of the individual artist who snatches from some remote inspiration a new revelation of truth and beauty.

3
AMERICA TAKES HOLD OF ITS DESTINY
Rexford Guy Tugwell*

Like Adolf Berle, Rexford Tugwell was teaching at Columbia University when he joined Roosevelt's team in 1932. In many respects Tugwell was the most radical of the brains trusters. But while he believed that the Marxist critique of capitalism was largely correct and that some form of collectivism would replace free competition, Tugwell stopped short of advocating socialism. His association with Roosevelt in the campaign, he recalled later, persuaded him that America's "pluralistic arrangements" were incompatible with any sort of "monolithic economy." Consequently, if social reformers expected to change things for the better, they would have to work within existing institutions. After Roosevelt's election Tugwell held various posts in the Department of Agriculture and served for a year as Resettlement Administrator. His academic background and unorthodox beliefs, however, made him a favorite target of conservatives, and in 1936 he left office. During the spring of 1934 Tugwell set forth his conviction that America was moving gradually toward a "realm of cooperative plenty." What kind of "radical changes" in values and institutions did Tugwell consider necessary? What assumptions about economic policy did he share with Berle, and where did they differ? Why did Tugwell prefer control to competition, what dangers did he detect in such a policy, and how did he think they could best be averted? While Tugwell's article illustrates the way in which the early New Deal buoyed the hopes of democratic collectivists, it also points up their dilemma: If radical changes were truly necessary, could they take place within the existing institutional framework and without a fundamental alteration in the distribution of power between various groups in society? □

The real economic revolution is just beginning in the United States.

It is a fundamental error to assume that we have reached the end of the "swing to the left," and that we may forego any further important policy changes.

---

*Tugwell, Rexford Guy, America Takes Hold of Its Destiny, *Today,* I (April 28, 1934), 7, 22-23. Copyright *Newsweek,* Inc., 1934. Reprinted by permission.

I have little patience with those who say that we have come to the end of a period of progress; that we must now retrench and economize, hoarding our gains against a poverty-stricken future.

One of our troubles has been that we have hoarded and economized too much, rather than devoting ourselves to organizing and expanding our resources and capabilities. We do not seem to realize that it is our own abundance which compels us to make radical changes, first in our ideas and then in the institutions based on our ideas.

This is as true of government as of individuals. As individuals, we are apt to ride in airplanes with horse-and-buggy ideas in our heads. And our government has done the same thing. It has attempted to function in a world which has long since outgrown it.

All the prejudices and shibboleths which survive in people's heads seem to crystallize in government—perhaps because, very rightly, we think of it as somehow sacred. But it will not stay sacred long if it is set apart from change in a changing world. It simply will become atrophied and obsolete, and will either be ignored or contemptuously brushed aside by those in the community who have important affairs afoot which they desire shall not be interfered with.

Something like this has been happening to our government. I think it fair to say that until March, 1933, it was fast becoming ineffectual in its relationships with industry. It insisted on an interpretation of industrial life belonging to an era which had disappeared.

It broke up trusts as a sufficient answer to the pressing problem of control; and when it discovered that the more they were broken up the more they remained as they had been, it fell into a kind of trance. It was unwilling to give up competitive theory; it could therefore think of nothing to do except to restore competition; and when competition refused to be restored, industry continued to exist in a kind of purgatory—half the heaven of freedom and half the hell of ineffectual public disapproval.

The various recovery acts proceeded from a theory in sharp contrast to all this.

SECURING INDUSTRY'S BENEFITS

This theory recognized the changes which had occurred in industrial society, and it sought to secure the benefits of industry as it actually existed for the public good.

"Industry," it said, "has developed out of the face-to-face stage; huge factories exist; central-office organizations even control many of these organizations, great as they are in themselves; financial controls are superimposed on this; scientific management has come to stay—therefore the government must legalize all these heretofore horrid developments so that it may shape them into social instruments."

In effect, this was the theoretical basis of the recovery program. The Sherman Act and the Clayton Act were not repealed; but insofar as the codes could become effective, their operation was suspended.

The codes now have become operative over most of industry; and it can be said that we have turned our backs on competition and have chosen control. This transformation, very nearly complete as it is, provides, as I believe, an instrument suitable to the purpose of enriching our life as it is our ambition to do.

With this instrument we can, for the first time, proceed to the management of purchasing power. And when purchasing power is provided, the potentialities of our vast producing equipment can be released. It is toward this that we have been working. It would be folly to assume that, having created the means towards our chosen end, we should forego the end for which these means were created.

To suggest, therefore, that it is time to call a halt on the application of social control to the physical distribution of American abundance, is on a par with that old legislative spirit which decreed that no man should drive an automobile on a public highway unless he were preceded by another man afoot, carrying a red flag to warn pedestrians to keep out of the way.

The New Order is conceived in no such spirit of obscurantism. It is a beginning, not an end.

This new legislation is best described in some such terms as this—as a charter for experiment and research, for invention and learning. The new institutions have not sprung fullgrown from these legislative acts—the Agricultural Adjustment Act, National Recovery Act and the rest—any more than the original government of the United States sprang fullgrown from the Constitutional Convention.

They mark a turning point, just as that convention did. We had to learn about democratic government in practice; we had to grow into it by trying various devices and by learning to live together within a new framework. The same thing is true of this better planned society we are entering upon now.

In both cases, we expressed a determination to go forward in a general direction and within an agreed framework of rules, but without specific commitment to policies concerning problems which could not yet be foreseen. In entering on such an untrod path, it is unwise to lay down too specifically the structure of new things; it always is better merely to register a change of heart and mind and then begin to work out, patiently and carefully, the requirements of the conversion.

No one could have foreseen at first in what the processes of code and agreement-making would result. Even now, no one can foresee the final structure of industry which may result. Whatever it may be, it will be worked out by the essentially voluntary and democratic processes now going on.

But we can begin, at least, to look forward to the time when the preliminary structure will be complete. Every industry then will have set up a kind of government of its own, within which those aims which it holds in common can be pressed for, and those discords and controversies which exist can be compromised and mediated. It was necessary to pass through this rather protracted period of conflict and discussion before these industrial groups could be ready for planning.

WASTING ENERGY IN COMPETITION

Up to now, much of the energy of business men has been dissipated in over-praised conflicts of competition. Each was trying to beat the other fellow—to reach success by standing on the exhausted bodies of fallen competitors. The success for which all this striving took place was usually defined as the right to exploit consumers by selling them goods of doubtful quality at prices which lowered the general standard of living.

This competition is being outlawed. Code-making, if it had done nothing else, would have been worth while for the revelation it has given our industrialists of the essential futility of much of their activity. We are fast approaching the time, therefore, when each industry will be able to devote its best energy to the fundamental purpose of industry—which is production, rather than competition. Already this has gone far enough so that some of the problems which will be involved in the next stage of progress are beginning to be disclosed.

At the first stage, it has seemed to many business men—and this is why they consented to be drawn in at all—that if they and their immediate rivals could mitigate their differences, and if they could combine even in informal ways, the obstacles to price-fixing might be removed; and since every business man always has lived under the immediate and intense pressure of prices, this seemed wholly good.

Some of us have foreseen the difficulties which would arise at this stage, and these have given us a key to the next major development of public policy, so we have pressed continually for a double check to be applied when the time should come—both for the protection of the consumer—a check on quality and a check on prices.

This protection of the consumer was not conceived merely in the consumer's interest. It was rather in the interest of a continuous and permanent economic organization that it was desired to oppose the consumer's interest to that of the producer, or, more accurately, the principle of value to the principle of profit, in the interest of a sustained and adequate purchasing power which could absorb the products of industry and agriculture.

Industry cannot permanently base itself on public deception. It cannot even keep running unless it provides, through decent wage policies and rigorously lowered prices, for continuing customers. And this is the next problem which has to be faced—the one which will be most prominent in public discussion during the months to come. We now have ended the stealthy robbery of a rigid monetary standard; we must proceed to end the robbery of consumer deception.

The industrialist who went into code and agreement-making with the idea that he had found an excellent device for exploiting the public is apt to be disillusioned pretty rapidly. He had, of course, a line of defense to fall back on—but one which will not stand exposure any better than will shoddy goods or extortionate prices.

This was the principle of limiting production. This is not a new idea either, any more than was the easy exploitation of consumers. For, it was said by industrialists, we will fix prices where we want them to be—where they will yield good, fat profits—and then we will make only as much goods as the public will take at that price.

The difficulty with this principle, heretofore, has been the danger that someone who could do the job as cheaply, or perhaps cheaper, would come into the market and undersell the price-fixer. One reason why the codes looked good to business men was the chance they saw of outlawing this competition. If the fellow who was willing to sell better or cheaper goods could be kept out, their own poorer or more expensive goods would have all the market there was.

It is undeniable, I think, that some of the codes already have been used in this way and that we are worse off, rather than better off, in a permanent sense, because of them.

But grave difficulties have arisen. Industries sell not only to gullible individual consumers; they sell to one another. And buyers, in this case, know the game as well as sellers do. So that even before the completion of the code structure, there was a sharp challenge to the policy of limitation.

There already is great resistance from industrial consumers. Indeed, there is a kind of game now going on, which must be amusing to some sardonic bystanders, in which some industries try to prevent others from doing what they themselves are making the most determined efforts to do. It is part of the nature of this process that all these chiselers must discover that only by subordination of their particular ambitions to those of all, can they continue to exist in passable peace. The thing will iron itself out in the processes now going on.

This reconciliation of differences, however quickly it may come, or whatever contractual relationships it establishes among industries, is not, however, sufficient. For there always remains the essentially defenseless ultimate consumer. The government may turn out to be his only refuge; and if this is so, the government will have to assume more and more responsibility for pushing his case.

There are two broad ways in which industrial policy may be shaped from this point on to secure this objective.

Industry may be required to define the quality of the goods offered and to sell them at prices which are suitably low, so that when the transactions of a year, for instance, are totaled up, it will be found that our energies and our producing plants have been used to the utmost and that the goods and services they yield have gone to consumers without increase of debt.

Or industry may be allowed to proceed with the policy of establishing high prices and maintaining them by limitation, and of selling goods whose qualities are mysterious to most consumers; and much of the resulting profits may be taken in taxes and returned to consumers as free goods by the government—in the form of facilities for health and recreation, insurance against old age, sickness and unemployment, or in other ways.

CHOOSING AN ECONOMIC POLICY

We shall have to accept one or the other of these policies, because, if we do not, we shall sacrifice most of those objectives we associate with what has been called the New Deal.

The choice which lies before us is, therefore, a choice between a socially wise economic policy and the application of socialistic taxation. I prefer the former method.

One of the distinguishing characteristics of the present is the power of our industrial machine to produce goods. This power has astonished and frightened us. We have not known what to do about it. It required that we should chain it up and prevent its free functioning or that we should reorganize our machinery of distribution so that consumers could take possession of the vast flow of goods.

If we are to accept, fairly and squarely, the consequences of what we have done in the way of invention, the perfecting of new processes, scientific management, transport and communication, these arrangements must be made, consisting in freer access to the goods which are made.

To enter on a policy of limitation is really to deny the best work of the last fifty years. If we are to do this, it would be more consistent to go back to where we were—to scrap machines and processes, to exile, execute or imprison our inventors and engineers, to depend once more on hand work, to use less power, and generally to stop the flow of goods at the source. Otherwise we shall have to resort permanently, as we are doing now in emergency cases, to limitation of hours, making unnecessary work, and letting our magnificent plants stand idle.

This would not be progress, as we understand it; it would be an admission that we have created a Frankenstein which we are unable to master.

It is my belief that we will prove unwilling to accept limitation in this sense as a permanent policy. This does not mean that we may not plan; it does not mean that we may not choose to use our resources in one way rather than another, limiting in some instances and expanding in others, so that all may run smoothly together as a considered and coordinated whole. That industry shall choose to proceed in this fashion is extremely important; and this is why it is necessary that all industry shall begin to function as soon as possible under the codes.

Furthermore, we shall not know to what lengths government will have to go until it is seen whether industry is capable, under the new dispensation, of arranging itself so that the full resources of our productive capacities can be used. For the first time, it is being provided with an adequate organization for accepting its obligations. It remains to be seen whether these responsibilities will be met in fact. If they are not, and if the objectives of the New Order are to be achieved, there will be a greater governmental task to be done than is foreseen at present.

It is, as I conceive it, better that industry shall try for itself to find the road to continuity; it is better also that such price and wage policies shall be adopted as will insure the full and free flow of goods into the hands of consumers. Only in this way can the rising demand for governmental intervention be stifled.

Intervention would be bound to interfere with efficiency. Many of the controls would necessarily be negative. A great deal of otherwise unnecessary machinery would have to be set up.

All this would be very expensive and repressive. But if industry, working, as it now has the chance to do, in cooperation with government, will adopt policies of low prices, high wages and a planned use of its capacity, foregoing speculative profits in some periods as well as speculative deficits in succeeding ones, all the objectives will have been accomplished. This would, in fact, be a new kind of government.

Using the traditional methods of a free people, we are going forward toward a realm of cooperative plenty the like of which the world never has seen. It will be no antiseptic utopia and no socialistic paradise, but a changing system in which we can live changing lives.

I have tried to make it clear that the objectives and the instruments being used in the reconstruction which is now going on are novel only in the sense that they are devices which have not hitherto been used.

I also have stressed their experimental nature. That seems to me their most important characteristic, and that is something which is American, if anything is—at least, there was a time when Yankee ingenuity was a by-word of praise.

I have been too closely associated with all that has taken place to be an impartial witness; nevertheless, I cannot help feeling that the nation has taken hold of its destiny again in ways which show that we have not lost our courage and resourcefulness. It was simply stifled for a while. There is no reason to think that year by year we shall not learn to better ourselves with the full use of energies and instruments which we have at our disposal.

If this be Socialism, let our enemies make the most of it!

4
GOVERNMENT AND BUSINESS
Thurman Arnold*

In 1935, after experiments with industrial planning had proved disappointing (or had been declared unconstitutional by the Supreme Court), the Roosevelt administration launched the Second New Deal. Inclined more toward competition then concentration, this approach was symbolized by the breakup of holding companies in public utilities, the investigation of monopoly power by the Temporary National Economic Committee, and the appointment of Thurman Arnold to head the Justice Department's Anti-Trust Division in March, 1938. In *The Folklore of Capitalism,* which was published in 1937 while he was teaching at the Yale Law School, Arnold had ridiculed previous efforts to enforce the Sherman Act. Nevertheless he rapidly became the New Deal's most vigorous trustbuster. From 1939 through 1941 the Anti-Trust Division filed no less than 180 complaints. Arnold's economic theory rested on the distinction he found between two worlds: one of organized, monopolistic industry and the other of small businessmen, farmers, workers, and consumers. To what extent do Arnold's views reflect the tradition of Louis D. Brandeis, Woodrow Wilson and the New Freedom? Does he believe that trusts are in any sense immoral or inevitably harmful? Upon what criteria does he base his decisions? Arnold maintains that the United States must avoid centralized government control of centralized economic power; but do his fears resemble those of Berle and Tugwell? Arnold never retreated from his endorsement of the experimental, pragmatic character of Roosevelt's policies. In his autobiography (1965), Arnold reflected, "The most dangerous President that America could have had during the time of the Depression would have been a man who thought he understood and honestly tried to follow any form of consistent economic doctrine, whether liberal or conservative." Does the New Deal experience justify this assessment? ☐

---

*Arnold, Thurman W., Feathers and Prices, *Common Sense,* VII (July, 1939), 3-6.

The tendency in public discussion of the relation of government to business is to soar off the earth like a balloon. If you attempt to say everything about everything, you end by saying nothing about anything. As William James once put it—to the practical man, such discussions are tedious, not as hard subjects like physics and mathematics are tedious, but as throwing feathers endlessly, hour after hour, is tedious.

I am not an inspirational preacher. I am unskilled in throwing philosophical feathers. Therefore I shall leave the more general treatment of the questions which are discussed today and attempt to be concrete.

At a recent conference attended by legal and economic scholars in connection with the monopoly inquiry, someone suggested that the first step was to think the thing through and decide whether we want a competitive system, and if so what kind. A similar thought was expressed by Charles Beard in *The New Republic* last year, when he wrote:

> I have come to the conclusion that ours is now and in the nature of things is destined to be, a great continental, technological society, and that the trustbusters however honest and honorable, are just whistling in the wind, as Senator Platt said in 1890—are prolonging the dangerous tension in American society, are unwittingly the foes of getting our economic machine in full motion, and are destined to defeat besides. The only unsettled question in my mind now is whether they will be able to defeat or postpone heroic action on a continental scale long enough to bring ruin down upon all of us.

I am convinced that America is not yet ready to accept "heroic action on a continental scale." I believe that if we take up our problems, industry by industry, case by case, in a spirit which is based on the competitive ideal, but which is willing to take such limited measures of control as hard facts (not principles) indicate, we can avoid imposing an alien tradition on our competitive economy.

If we are going to get anywhere, we must talk about one thing at a time. Otherwise we get lost in a maze of Utopian planning which has no relationship to actual political possibilities.

There are many ways of describing the problem which confronts us.

Look at it in terms of production. It is undisputed that we might have produced in the past ten years much more goods and services than we did produce. The conservative Brookings Institution estimates the economic loss due to our failure to use our productive plant to capacity amounted during a ten year period to the colossal sum of 248 billion dollars. This amounts to $8,000 a family—more than 90 per cent of our families could save in a lifetime. This is dangerous kind of waste because it presents to those in need the spectacle of goods withheld from them for no understandable reason.

Look at it in terms of distribution. Most of our advertised price levels are based on the assumption that the ordinary family gets somewhere between $2500 and $5000 a year. Actually only 13% are above the $2500 family income level. This is less than the population of the state of New York. We cannot produce goods for a country the size of America and base the distribution of them on the population of a single state.

Look at it in terms of a national or per capita income. In the year 1938 we descended to the income level of nearly 20 years ago in spite of our vastly increased productive wealth.

I have elsewhere referred to our economic structure as consisting of two separate worlds. The first is a world of organized industry, the second a world of small unorganized business, farmers, laborers and consumers. In the first world, there is the power to maintain high prices no matter how much the demand for the product falls off. The result is that production drops, men are laid off and this in turn lowers the purchasing power and makes the demand drop still further. In the second world, unlimited competition still exists and cannot be controlled. In this world live the farmers, retailers, and the small business men who supply the consumers with both goods and labor. Here, when the supply increases or the demand falls off, prices drop to the bottom, but the people go right on producing as much as the conditions of the market will permit.

The trouble with the system is that the first of these worlds works at cross purposes with the second. In the first world, great organizations keep up prices and lay off labor. The labor so laid off has no power to purchase the consumer goods furnished by the second world.

In solving the difficulties created by these two worlds, the government is stepping into the breach today to provide the second or competitive world with more purchasing power. It is spending money on relief, and to aid home owners, and in new construction. It attempts to raise wages from starvation levels and to help farmers maintain crop prices which will give them enough purchasing power to buy the goods of the first world of organized industry. But this can never succeed if the world of organized industry maintains and raises prices faster during the period of adjustment than the government supplies temporary purchasing power. That process drains away the money from those who receive it from the government, and then stops the circulation of the money by failing to distribute goods and by laying off men who should be consuming what the industry produces.

It is my conviction that we are being forced to abandon our former policy of easy acquiescence in industrial empire building, because of the failure of great industrial empires to adapt their price policies, so that they can distribute the goods which they are capable of making and so that they can employ labor and run their plants at capacity. The recent depression brought home to us the absurdity of people going without goods because inventories of these very goods had become too large. Production had to stop and men were discharged at a scale new in our history. This was followed by a demand for an investigation of the monopoly practices and price policies which stopped the flow of goods by destroying the purchasing power of consumers and small business men. We are being forced to take control of inflexible price structures and coercions in restraint of trade today, just as in 1933 we were forced to take control of the financing and marketing of securities.

WHY THE TRUSTS WEREN'T BUSTED

The anti-trust laws have been on the books for over forty years. During this period, we have always been just about ready to enforce them. We have written books; we have passed supplemental legislation; we have preached; we have defined; we have built a great system of legal metaphysics; and we have denounced. Indeed, we have done everything except to get an organization together and do an actual practical job of policing.

In the era of Theodore Roosevelt trust-busting was supposed to be at its height. To read the history of that time is to get the impression that anti-trust enforcement was one of the principal activities of government. How many employees were engaged in it? The personnel of the Anti-Trust Division during that famous crusade consisted of only five lawyers and four stenographers. When this administration came into office, there were only 15 lawyers. Today, it has been increased to about 90. This small group is supposed to police the enforcement of a law covering the industrial activity of 130,000,000 people. By contrast, the Securities and Exchange Commission has eight regional offices and a personnel of over 1,200.

The enforcement of the antitrust laws in the past has been a series of crusades. A crusade is concerned more with the dramatization of an ideal than with continuous practical control. So long as the personnel of the Department is so small that violations of the antitrust laws must be ignored, because there is no one to investigate or try them, we have no practical control of the situation.

Another difficulty has arisen from the practice of lumping dissimilar situations together. Suppose that you attempted to treat tourists and elephants and trees in the same way because they all had trunks. You would immediately become lost in metaphysics. If someone objected that their trunks were of different kinds, you could immediately reply that essentially they were all the same. They were all used to carry things. The elephant's trunk carried hay to the elephant's mouth, the tourist's trunk carried clothing, and the trunk of the tree carried sap for the leaves. This would satisfy the legal scholar. However, the regulations which you drew as a result of that process would not be practically effective. This method, without any exaggeration whatever, is one which we drift into when we divorce definition of the antitrust law from actual enforcement and application to concrete industries.

Everyone is asking me to define a monopoly. Antitrust laws are often referred to as anti-monopoly laws. The term is misleading. Restraints of trade which create inflexible price structures, coercion of competitors and the closing of economic opportunity by forceful means are found everywhere, in small as well as large concerns. The only reason that large businesses have been featured so exclusively in antitrust administration is the fact that shortage of funds and personnel have prevented the Department of Justice from taking up the smaller violators.

As a generalization it is as meaningless to say that small units are better than big units as to say that small buildings are better than big ones, or low buildings better than high ones. Such statements are on a par with saying that Milton is more poetical than the pig is fat. When applied to concrete situations these metaphysical differences disappear. The question as to which side of the line any particular industry falls can be determined not by arguing conflicting principles but by factual investigation.

The preventive enforcement of the antitrust laws lies in criminal enforcement. However, anti-trust offences are not ordinary criminal offences. Business is not carried on by the criminal classes. In the past the concentration of economic power has been treated as a moral question. The issue has been confused by the notion that we are trying to determine whether great business organizers were bad men or good men.

It is important, therefore, to recognize that antitrust enforcement is not a moral problem. It is the problem of continuous direction of economic traffic. It is not solved by preaching. It requires an adequate organization to penalize those who are reckless or in too much of a hurry. The competitive struggle without effective antitrust enforcement is like a fight without a referee. In such a contest, the man who puts on brass knuckles will win. This situation will not be solved by hanging mottoes of fair play on the four posts of the ring.

In addition to enforcement measures, however, cases where some sort of combination or concerted action by business men is necessary, because of particular situations, require a constructive solution. It is the lack of understanding of the constructive use of the antitrust laws which has led to the impression today that the Sherman Act was passed to commemorate Sherman's march to the sea.

The economic necessities of a machine age require that we recognize three principles in the application of the law. These principles may be stated as follows: (1.) Combinations which actually contribute to the efficiency of mass production should not be destroyed. (2.) Concerted action on the part of groups of competitors in order to insure orderly marketing conditions should not be considered unreasonable. (3.) The third situation to which the rule of reason must be applied has been created by our lack of enforcement in the past. A short phrase to describe it would be to call it the problem of unscrambling the eggs. Where competition has been destroyed no imposition of penalties can re-create it.

A constructive application of the antitrust laws requires informing business men what they *may* do in their own industries where these principles are involved. Penalties look at the past. They must be supplemented by a guide for the future.

As an example take the puzzling problem of the price policies in the heavy industries. Examine the tangle of goods and services which go to make up a house. No one makes an entire house, therefore a drop in structural steel or cement will not of itself affect the price of the building. Suppose, however, that all the industries which contribute to housing should bring down their prices together. In that case we might expect the price of the house itself to come within the reach of a substantial majority of our population. The drop in prices should be rewarded by an increased demand.

A price reduction of this kind requires concerted action. To make concerted action possible, there must be a method to inform business men what they may do. The sporadic attempts made in the past to do this by a quasi-promise of immunity from prosecution were a conspicuous failure.

Another method must be found, a method of giving approval to orderly marketing practices designed to lower prices.

To sum up, I recognize the necessity of large organizations in order to attain efficient mass production. I recognize that trust-busting for the mere sake of breaking up large units is futile, if those units are justified in terms of efficiency. Nevertheless, these obvious facts should not be made the excuse for industrial empire building.

It is my hope that we are not going to drift through the channels of centralized industrial power into the harbor of centralized Government control of that power. We have gone far along that road. In 1933 over 50% of all net corporate income was earned by less than one-tenth of 1% of the corporations reporting and 84% of the aggregate corporate net profits was earned by less than 4% of the corporations reporting. These are familiar figures often quoted. There are countless others showing the same tendency. Yet I am convinced that as yet they only represent a curable tendency.

If that hope is to be realized, however, we must take practical steps to that end. Preaching and denunciation of totalitarian systems of industrial control is as useless as preaching against disease. We have seen the dictatorial governments of today grow stronger each year under that type of treatment. Dictatorships flow in like water into a vacuum where those formerly in control of an economic system drop the reins of power and preach instead of taking action to meet the immediate needs of the time.

The inevitable end of industrial control by private combinations, cartels and trade associations is illustrated by Germany today. Prior to the war that country had no antitrust law, but industrial self-regimentation was counter-balanced by a strong centralized government, ready to adopt necessary socialistic legislation. In the depression that followed the war, a weak government in Germany permitted the self-regimentation of industries to proceed without restriction. Public discontent forced the enactment in 1923 of a decree similar in purpose to our antitrust law. But unfortunately for Germany its tradition of free enterprise was too weak. The law was never enforced. The year 1927 witnessed the last gasp of free enterprise in Germany. An Imperial Economic Commission was appointed to study the monopoly problem. It sat for three years, produced nearly 40 volumes, and ended on the note of letting business combinations alone.

With this encouragement German business regimentation drifted to its logical conclusion: There was only one answer. Germany was organized to such an extent that it needed a general and Hitler leaped into power. Had it not been Hitler it would have been someone else.

We may as well admit that monopolies controlled by an efficient centralized government really interested in increasing the production and distribution of goods *can* be used to advance business recovery. They stifle free and independent enterprise, but they lend themselves to the army system of control. It is becoming quite obvious today that armies are not inefficient and that an industrial structure *can* be governed on military principles. Indeed, it is amazing to contemplate Germany's defeat in the World War, followed twenty years after by Munich.

I assume, however, that the American people want recovery under a system of free, independent and competitive enterprise. We do not want the vast extension of state control necessary to make a monopoly economy work. We recognize the necessity of regulated public utilities where monopoly control creates efficiency but we do not wish to extend the area of government regulation any further than necessary. These assumptions do not need elaboration because they represent our most deep rooted American tradition. To abandon that tradition would require a reversal of all our economic ideals. I know of no important American political group prepared to abandon these ideals.

The confusion, hatreds and bitterness which accompany the rise of new institutions, to fill gaps which established institutions are unable to fill, constitute part of the growing pains of civilization.

The commonplace individuals whom Chance designates as leaders to control any social organization must be clothed in some sort of uniform to conceal the fact that they are like other men. The uniform of a democracy is made of the words and principles we've been brought up to like. I would be the last to prefer one of more military design to the uniform which gives ordinary persons like me their power. In the struggle for progress I prefer that the weapons be words, not guns.

PART TWO
THE CONSERVATIVE RESPONSE

5
THE COMING AMERICAN FASCISM
Lawrence Dennis*

The decade of the 1930's gave rise to a certain amount of fascist sentiment in the United States. Several would-be fuehrers—including George Deatherage of the Knights of the White Camelia, William Dudley Pelley of the Silver Shirts, and Colonel Eugene Nelson Sanctuary of the American Christian Defenders—claimed that the New Deal was at bottom a Jewish and Communist plot to seize control of America. Taking Italy and Germany as their models, native fascists seem to have appealed primarily to members of the lower middle class who had been hard hit by the depression and were prepared to think in either paranoid or conspiratorial terms. But there was another strain of fascist thought which had a more theoretical appeal. Its chief spokesmen were Seward Collins, editor of *The American Review,* and Lawrence Dennis, a graduate of Exeter and Harvard who had served during the 1920's as a foreign service officer in Latin America. Dennis believed that fascism, as the system which would guarantee order and efficiency, would win the support of the elite. The wealthiest and best educated quarter of the American people, he asserted, had "a class consciousness, pride, and solidarity which the proletarians lack." The masses, moreover, had no attachment to abstractions like "liberty" and "democracy." "All of these words or symbols can be incanted by any demagogue" who would promise the people "public order and the elements of subsistence." Dennis also admitted to a fear that American

---

*Dennis, Lawrence, *The Coming American Fascism.* New York: Harper and Bros., 1936, vii-xi, 163-81, abridged. Reprinted by permission of Lawrence Dennis.

fascism might be "tainted with some of the unfortunate race and religious prejudices now cherished by large numbers of our people." In 1936 Dennis published *The Coming American Fascism;* 35 years later he claimed that "the book was not advocacy but prediction on my part." The following selections explain why Dennis saw in fascism the wave of the future. □

INTRODUCTION

This book is addressed to the thoughtful who are not frightened by new and unpopular terms and concepts. If liberal capitalism is doomed, a fight for a lost cause will impose on mankind the most futile sort of suffering. The British Mercantilist System of the 18th Century and the Southern Planter-Slavery System of the pre-industrial-revolution period each fought on American soil an utterly futile and foolish war to save what was doomed by the inevitable and irresistible trend of social changes. If the present system, or more particularly, those features of it which are challenged by current trends be doomed, the longer and harder the fight waged to preserve it, the greater will be the suffering and losses of the people. Assuming that the old system is doomed, the basic premise of this book and an assumption which current events surely render probable enough to be entertained as an hypothesis in exploratory thinking about the near future, What are the possible alternatives to ultimate social disintegration and chaos? Most intelligent observers of the changing scene, whatever their personal preferences and prejudices, are agreed that, in the event the present system is not soon made to work better, the alternatives fall into the broad classifications of fascism or communism. . . .

Both fascism and communism should be thought of as formulas of revolutionary social action for those of the underprivileged, dissatisfied and frustrated who have a will to power and a will, through the seizure and use of power, to change a situation they find intolerable, and, of course, to conserve a situation they find more satisfactory. Both fascism and communism are crisis formulas, that is to say, unlike formulas of liberal reform, neither has significance except in so far as it may have a chance of full realization as a new totalitarian or all-embracing social scheme. And, unlike liberal reform, neither has such a chance except in measure as the crisis of the existing system makes an entirely different system the alternative to chaos.

While fascism is to be thought of essentially as a formula for the frustrated in an extreme social crisis, it also has a strong appeal to many whose personal fortunes may still be far from desperate in such a crisis, as well as to national governments which may be interested more in conservation than further acquisition. Such persons, while moved by no feeling of frustration, still do not feel a zest for, or confidence in the outcome of, any fight to the finish under present world conditions between those in the house of want and those in the house of have. Interestingly enough, large numbers of extreme conservatives seem to share the understandable eagerness of the extreme communists for such a fray. The communists are entirely logical and loyal to self-interest in desiring and promoting wherever and whenever possible an intensification of class warfare. From it they have nothing to lose and, as a result of it, a chance to come to full power. The back-to-Hoover Republicans or back-to-Jefferson Democrats who would liquidate the New Deal or the back-to-liberalism British leaders who would liquidate fascism in international war stand only to lose by fighting those in the house of want, be they underprivileged nations seeking a place in the sun or the frustrated élite in liberal countries seeking an escape from the consequences of indefinitely prolonged depression. It is little short of astounding to see how the liberals of Downing Street, Wall Street and the Quai d'Orsay have been welcoming the comradeship in sanctions and arms of communist Russia against fascist Italy. (The fountain head of liberalism in America is really Wall Street or the eastern plutocracy, with its endowed and kept agencies of liberal indoctrination, the leading colleges and metropolitan newspapers.) These moneyed liberals who are seeking to use communist Russia in a war against fascism are singularly blind to their own interests, since they can never be comrades of communists. The liquidation of fascism where it is in power could only mean the succession of communism, and that could only mean the liquidation before a firing squad of property owners. And it is not to be supposed by the liberals of England, France, or even the United States, that they would long be safe in a world half-communist. The fact, of course, is that the liberals and conservatives, really two terms for the same people nowadays, as a whole, are still not sufficiently worried over the implications of present trends or over the ability of the system to stage a come-back. To those still in the house of have who are worried and humanely disposed at the same time, fascism makes an appeal which communism cannot make. Fascism does not expropriate all property rights or effect a wholesale liquidation of the owning and managing classes of the present order. And fascism does not mean a dictatorship by the leaders of the Marxist parties, falsely called by the communists a dictatorship of the proletariat. . . .

WHY FASCISM INSTEAD OF COMMUNISM?

. . . We shall assume that an ideal fascism for America must provide for maximum economic production and consumption with a steady rise in living standards and a progressive expansion of productive plant, all without either a class or civil war or the expropriation of all private rights in the instruments of production. The alternatives of such a formula seem to be only those of making liberal capitalism work better or accepting communism, the emergence of a triumphant dictatorship of the proletariat from a bloody class war and expropriation of all private property rights in producers goods. It is appropriate at this point in the discussion to undertake some explanation why the fascist formula seems preferable to the communist formula. This explanation is particularly indicated in connection with a statement of the radical ends and means embraced in the fascist plan.

Now the ideals of order and planned abundance are not, as ideals, peculiar to fascism, liberal capitalism, or communism. Many readers will undoubtedly find fault with this book for not being a detailed outline of a fascist utopia and for having too much to say in the abstract about fundamentals, ends and means. The chief reason why so much is said about fascist social philosophy, and so little about an ideal or probable fascist handling of specific problems, is that it is mainly in the discussion of fascist philosophy that this book can be useful. Most socialists and radical would-be reformers within the liberal framework naïvely assume that the ideals of social order and welfare are peculiar to their philosophy, and they spend a lot of time telling us in glowing detail exactly what they would like to see happen, without conceiving that most people would also like to see these ideals realized. The problem is how to realize these ideals, and that problem is one of social engineering rather than technology. And when you talk social engineering, you must talk social philosophy before you can draw blue prints. . . .

There is reason to guess, on the basis of many estimates, that our productive plant could be made to furnish every family with an annual income of $5,000 within ten years of reasonable expansion and rationalization of industry. A minimum family income of $2,500 seems a comparatively easy objective for attainment within two or three years. . . .

Without piling fact on fact, or figure on figure, to support an obvious generalization, we may say that there can be no question either as to our need or capacity for increased production. The only real problem in this connection is that of mobilizing our productive factors and keeping them active. It is precisely at this point in the quest for planned abundance that fascism imposes itself as the only alternative to communism.

The choices we have are in the development of social machinery to make our material machinery give us the standard of living we desire. A fallacious assumption of all liberal reformism is that if the people can be induced to give, through a decisive majority vote, a mandate to their government to bring about some ideal measure of social justice and economic abundance, and if education and moral indoctrination inculcate the right attitudes, this mandate can be carried out within the framework of existing institutions and ways. To prove this assumption, they pile up irrelevant statistics and talk learnedly in the several jargons of the social and natural sciences. They quite simply do not take account of the fact that a better social order requires, in the field of social institutions, ways, attitudes, and mechanics, not only new objectives but a driving force, a guiding hand, and a coördinated system of control. Utopian wishes do not furnish a driving force. A series of majority votes arrived at by the parliamentary or Congressional methods of majority group pressures, lobbying, and the individual pursuit of reëlection by hundreds of office holders, do not constitute a guiding hand. And a political system of checks and balances is not coördinated control.

The driving force of any national undertaking may be called nationalism, patriotism, love of country, consciousness of kind, and loyalty to kind, or by any one of countless other terms or phrases. The reality which unites and animates a group in a feeling of solidarity, and in an enterprise of common interest, is too traditional, too universally felt and manifested, and too inevitable, to call for any attempt at exact definition. Communist Russia operates as a nation, and is driven by the dynamic force of national patriotism, or love of country and loyalty to kind, quite as much as any fascist country, or any liberal country in time of war. Little need be said by way of attempt to explain why and how this force will animate an American fascism. The generative sources of this force are inherent in every nation. It is necessary only to tap them and provide an orderly system through which they can flow. We do not need communism to get the forces of nationalism, and communism cannot provide a substitute for those forces.

Now communism professes to derive its driving force from the will of the workers to overthrow the rule of the owners of property, and substitute that rule with the dictatorship of the proletariat. As a matter of fact, of course, communism in operation has been a series of phenomena whose driving force has been derived from two main sources: First, the personal motivations, too complex always for brief analysis, of the initiating leaders–motivations springing from a sense of frustration under the existing order, feeling that this order was evil, and the love of power common to so many strong men; and, second, Russian patriotism, which was captured and mobilized by these initiating leaders of communism, exactly as French patriotism was captured and mobilized by a Corsican second lieutenant of artillery and soldier of fortune.

The class war, the classical myth of communism, like every other war, has been the war of one crowd against another. There is nothing much to starting or keeping up a war any more than there is to starting and keeping up a fire. It needs only the first spark and then plenty of fuel. The Communist ins, in Russia, have fought, and continue to fight, the outs. The ins of Russia would incite the outs of other countries to espouse the faith of the communist international and fight the ins of their respective countries. All this is simple. But nowhere is there apparent any significant manifestation of the driving force of a proletarian will to fight as proletarians, whether in Russia or anywhere else. Russia presents the spectacle of a national government on the defensive, just as do Britain, Germany, Japan and Italy, not the spectacle of a proletariat on the warpath against the capitalists of the world.

The choice between fascism and communism, then, turns largely around the questions of the inevitability and desirability from some assumed standpoint of the class war myth as a rationalization of what is just a war between two crowds, and, of course, of this war as an event. Here it may be said that the best way to start a revolution or civil war in the United States is not to use the Marxian class war myth. But more important still it may be said that it is not necessary to have a civil war in order to effect a social revolution. These two considerations seem rather effectively to eliminate communism as a desirable choice for any one who has not already been "converted" to communism.

Those who have not been converted to communism will do well to ask themselves these questions: Is such a war a necessary means to the end of a social order which will afford the people as a whole a better average life? Is such a war a necessary means to a good end for me as an individual?

The answer to the second question, of course, depends largely on who I am, or whether I should be among the liquidators or the liquidated. To answer the first question affirmatively, it must be assumed that a proletarian party will have the will to start such a war, the might to win it, and the competence, after they have won it, to run things more efficiently than the leaders or managers of the class they have liquidated could run things.

It is the last of these assumptions which is most open to challenge. The assumptions that a proletarian communist party can mobilize enough proletarian wills to fight the Marxian battle on the inspiration of the class war myth, and develop enough might to win the battle in the advanced industrial countries, can plausibly be ridiculed in the light of present indications. But no impregnable argument can be founded on such ridicule, for the wills of the masses can conceivably be changed quickly and galvanized into action for the pursuit of the maddest objectives—witness the Crusades.

It is the assumption that a proletarian party triumph in the classical Marxian battle could leave enough competent technicians unliquidated to run things in a way to maintain as high a living standard as could be maintained if these managing classes were allowed to function, which is open to the most effective challenge. And on that challenge much of the case for fascism rests.

In this connection it must be remembered that while the Russian communist revolution has liquidated several millions, it did not have to liquidate the same percentage or total number of middle class technicians found in the United States. Moreover, Russian economy was not as dependent on these middle class elements as are our economy and standard of living. And during the Russian communist experiment it has been found necessary to import foreign experts. In the field in which the class war in Russia has effected the most drastic or significant liquidation of people—agriculture—the output is lowest and still below pre-War levels.

Obviously, from the point of view of the interests of the owning and managing classes, there can be no question as to the undesirability of the communist civil war, which will necessarily mean for them liquidation—a euphemism for such experiences as being stood up against a wall and shot. It is from the point of view of the workers in the Marxian definition, or those whose income is not derived mainly from owning and managing productive property for a profit, that, for the sake of any possible argument, it has to be shown that the triumphant Marxian dictatorship will not yield advantages. It is most seductive to some workers to be told that they have a chance under communism to oust the present bosses and themselves become the bosses. Obviously this promise is a lie. For under communism the workers would merely have a different set of bosses.

There is no way of running industry without bosses, and there is no way of making every man his own boss. The only question of real interest to the masses is whether they would be better off to liquidate in communist fashion all the present bosses and proceed thereafter with new bosses developed under communism, or to try some social formula which would take advantage of the skills of the present bosses. Once the question is considered in this light, the answer is fairly obvious in countries like the United States, where a communist class war liquidation would deprive the country of some twenty millions of its workers out of a total of fifty million, these twenty millions including some six million farmers, all of whom are on the wrong side of the communist fence.

At this point a word should be said to refute a commonly made communist argument that most of the middle-class executives, experts, white collar workers, farmers and small enterprisers would go over to communism in the course of the class war and thus escape liquidation. This argument runs counter to any expectancy based on experience. When a fight starts, the lines between friend and foe are tightly drawn, and it rarely happens during a war that any significant number of those on one side of the line go over to the other. It is not in the nature of most people, especially most members of the middle classes, to prove turncoats in a fight. The longer and harder the Marxian class war, the greater would be the solidarity of the enemies of the communists. There is, of course, no doubt in any mind which thinks straight on this subject that a large percentage of the non-owning, non-managing, and non-enterprising workers would, in the United States, side in the Marxian war with the owners, managers, and enterprisers from the very start. Most of the American workers would side with the managers and enterprisers because of the force of tradition or attitudes formed by education and long habit and, also, because of the prestige or moral authority which the managing and owning classes deservedly enjoy in the United States where their competence is demonstrably superior to that of the élite of the Czarist régime of Russia.

We may conclude then that, because of the unavoidable liquidation of so many competent experts through a communist victory in the Marxian class struggle, the results would not be as favorable for the people as a whole, or even for the non-owning and non-managing workers, as a régime which required fewer human sacrifices to get started. But the driving force of a consciousness of group solidarity and common group objectives is needed to run the social machinery of any planned economy. If it is not the Marxian class war spirit, it must be some other martial spirit. This force fascism develops by intensifying the national spirit and putting it behind the enterprises of public welfare and social control.

Here fascism is not introducing a new force but merely intensifying a force inherent in every nation and putting this old force behind new public enterprises.

The unifying principle of national fellowship already exists. Unlike working class or proletarian class consciousness, it is not something which exists only by virtue of a logical classification of men into owners and workers. This Marxian classification is entirely valid for purposes of logic and definition. But it is a classification which no more creates two separate class consciousnesses or class identities for purposes of common thought and action than the division of all mankind into red heads and non-red heads.

Obviously, the more inclusive the unifying principle, the more conflict is avoided and the greater coöperation is achieved. Nationalism would be more inclusive in the United States than any formula of unity based on race, religion, profession or tastes. As Americans, we are all of one nationality, though not of one race, religion, profession or set of cultural tastes. Of course, a perfect internationalism would be still more unifying and inclusive. This consideration leads many humane minds to aspire to a social formula or unifying principle which would include all mankind or transcend national limitations. Here the inevitability of some limitation to the inclusiveness of a formula of social organization and operation is largely a matter of traditional imponderables and problems of sheer administration. If the world were to go one hundred per cent Communist or one hundred per cent Roman Catholic, any attempt at international unity would necessarily founder on the rocks of group traditions and in the complexities of administration, for which neither an international Communism nor an international Christianity would prove a solvent.

It is idle to hazard a speculation as to the possibility of ever effecting a workable formula of international unity in a distant future. It is worse than idle for any one nation to attempt to force on an unwilling world any ideal of international unity. If an international formula by universal assent is ever workable, it will not be necessary for any one nation to force any part of it on any other nation. And surely no one is interested in an international formula imposed and maintained by the might of one nation. Communism, of course, masquerades as an international formula to be made effective by the universal assent of the workers (thus eliminating international war) once the capitalists have been eliminated by the Marxian class war. But communism in action has developed no reasons for supposing that workers are any less Americans, Russians and Englishmen than capitalists.

In regard to the guiding hand and the mechanisms of social control necessary to a planned society, we may dispose at once of a great deal of confusion by saying that fascism and communism equally require centralized control. In the larger essentials of social control, so far as problems of technique, mechanism, and means are concerned, fascism and communism have many similarities. It is under this heading of the imperative principles and mechanisms of social control that it seems eminently fitting to compare fascism and communism in respect to private property rights, private initiative in production, profits, and the free market. It is understood, of course, that fascism stands for the maintenance of all these institutions. Here there is a real problem of choice. Fascism regards private property rights, private initiative, and the free market, subject to a proper régime of public interest, as useful institutions–useful means to public ends. The difference between fascism and liberalism, in this respect, is that fascism considers these institutions as means to national ends, whereas liberalism makes the nation and national government a means to the ends of private property and the free market. . . .

There is no need to expropriate private ownership of either savings or small scale enterprise in order to maintain adequate social control. It is necessary only to nationalize large financial institutions and monopolistic industries, as well as all corporations whose services are indispensable but whose management has become completely divorced from ownership, and to discipline adequately all private enterprises.

Wherever ownership and management have become separated, there is no good case to be made out for private ownership or private management. In these cases, ownership is held by an army of stockholders and bondholders, who cannot possibly have any say about the control and management exercised by self-perpetuating hierarchies of bankers, directors, and officials on the inside who are virtually irresponsible either to the owners or to the State for the results of their economic policies. Obviously, a governmental bureaucracy is preferable to a corporate bureaucracy, for the governmental bureaucracy can be made more responsible, more disciplined, and better integrated into a national plan. A corporate bureaucracy divorced from the control of owners is just a private army at the service of any pirate captain who may be made chief.

The fascist State can easily convert the great monopolies and bureaucratically-managed large corporations into State-controlled enterprises, the present owners and creditors of which will receive income bonds or shares in a government investment company and never know any practical difference between their present capitalistic relationship to the property and the relationship which a fascist State will define and maintain for them. The corporate bureaucracies, except for a few big shot men at the top, will never know the difference. For there is no real difference between being a yes-man official of a billion dollar bank and being an official of a State bureaucracy, except possibly as to compensation, and government owned or controlled corporations under fascism would allow generous compensation to efficient executives.

So far as considerations of efficiency are involved, almost any rational régime, either of complete government control or some modified government dictation of policies and management left in private managers' hands, would mean no greater or different administrative and practical difficulties than those already encountered under the bureaucratic management of self-perpetuating bank and corporate dictatorships. Actually, the management of all large corporations is wholly bureaucratic, subject only, as a practical matter, to the modifying dictation of big bankers and financial interests. Between the hierarchical bureaucracy of a political State and the hierarchical bureaucracy of a large corporation with its permanent dictator and his army of yes-men executives, there are no significant administrative or technical differences. In either case, all the advantages of owner-management are lacking and all the disadvantages of bureaucratic control are present. . . .

In so far as property rights and private enterprise are concerned, however, the strongest argument for fascism instead of communism may be found in the regulatory functions of an open market. The strongest criticism of any socialism of complete expropriation is that it leaves no free market, no pricing mechanism and no valid basis for economic calculation. Pure socialism is collective ownership and unified central direction of all material instruments of production which, sooner or later, must leave little or no freedom of choice for the individual as to consumption or occupation. . . .

The extreme liberal capitalist position that only effective demands made in a free market should be satisfied is equally untenable. There is a large field of economic goods in which production can be conducted by arbitrary assumption and dictation. Police protection, sanitation, public education, are goods which are already bought and paid for without any reference to market demand. Light and power, transportation, and basic foods and textiles in given but limited quantities, can be assumed necessary at an arbitrarily fixed price, and State intervention can insure the production of an adequate supply of these goods within an arbitrarily fixed price range for the common good. If there is a deficit it can be met by taxation—provided it is not too large. It is well to remember that it will never be possible for the State to have provided as much of everything as may be desired. Hence, there must be selection and rationing where arbitrarily determined production and prices are enforced. For the selection of goods to be produced at given costs, for sale at given prices, and in given quantities, and for the selection and combination of productive factors in producing these goods, the State must have the guidance of prices or values determined by a comparatively free market. It is impossible within the limits of a brief discussion to elaborate the reasons and examples showing why the control of freely made prices and competitively made profits are essential as guides, whether for State directives or private enterprise directives of production.

Fascism does not accept the liberal dogmas as to the sovereignty of the consumer or trader in the free market. It does not admit that the market ever can or should be entirely free. Least of all does it consider that market freedom, and the opportunity to make competitive profits, are rights of the individual. Some measure of market freedom, competition, private enterprise, and profits and losses for private enterprise, in the view of fascism, must be deemed essential as guides to any measure of social control.

Under fascism, private property, private enterprise, and private choice in the market, have no rights as ends in themselves. They have different measures of social usefulness subject to proper public control. If these institutions and ways are to have social utility to the State, the liberal régime must be ended, the great monopolies nationalized, and all the economic processes subjected to the discipline of a national plan. The ultimate objective is welfare through a strong national State, and neither the dictatorship of the proletarian nor the supremacy of private rights under any given set of rules.

6
PROGRESS TOWARD COLLECTIVISM
Albert Jay Nock*

Paradoxically, the author of one of the finest studies of Thomas Jefferson was a man who gradually lost faith in democracy. Albert Jay Nock, whose *Jefferson* was published in 1926, had served for several years as editor of *The Freeman* where he had elaborated an anti-statist philosophy that sometimes seemed to border on anarchism. While Nock disliked the manner in which businessmen and their Republican allies sought to use government for their own advantage in the 1920's, he was perhaps even more critical of the Roosevelt administration after 1933. Not only did he view the New Deal as a threat to individualism, but by then Nock had come to accept the elitist views of the architect Ralph Adams Cram. According to Cram, most men were really not human beings but rather some subspecies possessing "the limited, superstitious, second-rate proletarian mind." To Nock, therefore, the New Deal was merely part of a broader movement which included fascism and communism and which, under the auspices of a power-hungry demagogue, was making people into wards of the state. In 1935 Nock wrote *Our Enemy The State* and for several years thereafter contributed to the *American Mercury* a column denouncing the New Deal. By 1941 his articles had taken on anti-Semitic overtones which were echoed in his autobiography, *Memoirs of a Superfluous Man* (1944), published a year before his death. Some have recently suggested that there are points in common between Nock's anarchical anti-institutionalism and the critique of welfare state liberalism voiced by radicals in the late 1960's. Is there any merit in this view? What does Nock consider the true purpose of government, why has it been corrupted, what seems likely to follow from this corruption, and what is the prospect for reversing the trend? Is there any sense in which Nock's position cannot be construed as "conservative"? □

In conversation with me not long ago, one of my friends was speculating

---

*Nock, Albert Jay, Progress Toward Collectivism, *The American Mercury,* XXXVII (February, 1936), 168-74. Reprinted by permission of *The American Mercury.*

on what might have happened in 1932 if the government had taken a stand directly opposite to the one it did take. "Suppose, for instance," he said, "that in his inaugural address, Mr. Roosevelt had said: 'The banks are closed, and you are all looking to the government to open them again and get them going. You will look in vain. You think it is the first duty of a government to help business. It is not. The only concern that government has with banking or any other business is to see that it is run honestly, to punish any and every form of fraud, and to enforce the obligations of contract. This government has no concern with the present plight of the banks, except to see that any banker who acts dishonestly goes to jail–and to jail he shall go.' "

My friend thought that a good many people in the business world would have drawn a long breath of relief at the announcement of such a policy. They would cheerfully have said good-bye to their dollars that had been impounded or embezzled, for the sake of hearing that the government proposed thenceforth to keep hands strictly off business, except to see that it was run honestly; or in other words, that as far as business was concerned the government would limit itself strictly to making justice costless, accessible, sure, swift, and impartial. Aside from this it would leave business free to hoe its own row and get itself out of its own messes as best it might.

I did not agree. My belief was, and is that the business world would have acted like a herd of drug-addicts whose rations had been suddenly cut off, for in its relations with the government that is precisely what the representative business world of America has always been and is now–a herd of addicts. It has always believed that the one governmental function which dwarfs all others to insignificance is to "help business". Let any kind of industry get itself into any kind of clutter, and it is the government's duty to intervene and straighten out the mess. This belief has prevailed from the beginning; it has seeped down from the business world and pervaded the general population so thoroughly that I doubt whether there are five hundred people in the country who have any other view of what government is really for. It seems to me, therefore, as I said, that the abrupt announcement of a change of policy would have merely thrown the people *en masse* into the imbecile hysteria of hopheads who are bereft of their supplies.

This belief being as deeply rooted as it is–the belief that the one end and aim of government is to help business–the history of government in America is a history of ever-multiplying, ever-progressive interventions upon the range of individual action. First in one situation, then in another, first on this pretext, then on that, the government has kept continually stepping in on the individual with some mode of coercive mandate, until we all have come to think that invoking governmental intervention is as much the regular and commonplace thing as turning on water at a tap or throwing an electric-light switch. Professor Ortega y Gasset gives a good description of the American attitude towards the State. The ordinary man, he says, "sees it, admires it, knows that *there it is.* . . . Furthermore, the mass-man sees in the State an anonymous power and feeling himself, like it, anonymous, he believes that the State is something of his own. Suppose that in the public life of a country some difficulty, conflict, or problem, presents itself, the mass-man will tend to demand that the State intervene immediately, and undertake a solution directly, with its immense and unassailable resources." This is what America has always done. Moreover, apart from any public difficulty or problem, when the mass-man wants something very much, when he wants to get an advantage over somebody, or wants to swindle somebody, or wants an education, or a job, or hospital treatment, or even a handout, his impulse is to run to the State with a demand for intervention.

The thing to be noticed about this is that State intervention in business is of two kinds, negative and positive. If I forge a check, break a contract, misrepresent my assets, bilk my shareholders, or sophisticate my product, the State intervenes and punishes me. This is a negative intervention. When the State sets up a business of its own in competition with mine, when it waters down the currency, kills pigs, plows under cotton, labels potatoes; when it goes in for a Planned Economy or when it uses its taxing power to redistribute wealth instead of for revenue—that is, when it takes money out of other people's pockets merely to put it into mine, as in the case of the processing taxes, for example—that is a positive intervention. These two kinds of intervention answer to two entirely different ideas of what government is, and what it is for. Negative intervention answers to the idea expressed in the Declaration of Independence, that government is instituted to secure certain natural rights to the individual, and after that must let him strictly alone. It is exactly the idea attributed to the legendary King Pausole, who had only two laws for his kingdom, the first one being, *Hurt no man,* and the second, *Then do as you please.*

Positive intervention does not answer to this idea of government at all. It answers to the idea that government is a machine for distributing economic advantage, a machine for you to use, if you can get hold of it, for the purpose of helping your own business and hurting somebody else's. Pursuant to this idea of government, the machine is manned by a sort of prætorian guard, a crew of extremely low and approachable persons who are not there for their health, but because they are beset by the demons of need, greed, and vainglory. Then when I want an economic advantage of some kind, I join with others who have the same interest, and thus accumulate enough influence to induce the machine-crew to start the wheels going and grind out a positive intervention—a subsidy, land-grant, concession, franchise, or whatever it is that I and my group desire.

This latter idea of what government is for is the only one that ever existed in this country. The idea expressed by Mr. Jefferson in the Declaration, expressed in the clearest and most explicit language by Thomas Paine and Benjamin Franklin, did not last as long in the consciousness of America as a pint of whisky in a lumber camp. When Cornwallis disappeared from public view after the surrender at Yorktown, this idea also disappeared, never to return. Before the new government took its seat in 1789, the industrial interests were fully organized, ready, and waiting with a demand for positive intervention; and from that day to this, the demand for this, that, or the other positive intervention has gone on incessantly. This is what is actually meant by "helping business". None of the groups which dickers with the machine-crew for an intervention to help business really cares two straws about helping business. What they want is an intervention to help *their* business; and since positive State intervention cannot help them without hurting somebody else—for obviously no positive intervention can be good for everyone—it follows that they want that also.

Thus it has come to be accepted on all sides that government exists mainly for just this purpose. The securing of human rights, the cheap, prompt, and effective administration of justice—all this is regarded as secondary. In fact, we now see governments everywhere notoriously disregarding justice and human rights. Napoleon on St. Helena said that in fifty years all Europe would be either republican or cossack—well, here you have it. They show no concern with justice, but only with law—law which they themselves manufacture, mostly by irresponsible decree, or what in this country is called "executive order," to suit their own purposes. The American government has always been conspicuous for its indifference to justice, its disreputable subservience to expediency, its devotion to a corrupt and corrupting legalism. It started out that way, and with its steady progress in centralization, its steady accumulation of coercive power over more and more of the individual citizen's activities, its steady entrenchment of a larger and larger bureaucracy, it became steadily more indifferent, subservient, and corrupt, until it developed into the moral monstrosity that it now is. One hundred and thirty-five years ago, Mr. Jefferson said that if the American government ever became completely centralized, it would be the most corrupt on earth; and the single instance of the Maine campaign in 1934 is probably enough to show that it is now entitled to that distinction.

The perversion of the idea that government exists to help business is responsible for this. All a government can properly and safely do to help business is what the Declaration says it is supposed to do—maintain individual rights, punish any trespass on those rights, and otherwise let the individual alone. This would be a real help to business, and a great help. But this is not the idea and never has been. The idea, as I have said, is that the government should help some special business to the detriment of others, according as one or another person or group is able to influence the machine-gang to work the State machine for a positive intervention.

It is easy to see how serious collisions of interest are thus provoked. First, say, the steelmakers want an intervention. They run to the government about it. Then the textile people want one, then the glassmakers, then this-and-that type of industrialist follows suit. Then the shipping concerns and the railroads want interventions. They run to the government. Then the farmers want one, organized labor wants one, the ex-soldiers want one, the unemployed want one, the hoboes want one, and when each of these interests thinks it can muster force enough—force of numbers or of money or of political influence—to make an impression on the machine-crew, it runs to the government.

The technique of procedure is always the same. The machine-crew is a purely professional organization; it is interested in helping no business but its own. It does not care to listen to considerations of the general welfare of business or of anything else. Dealing with it is a pure matter of *quid pro quo.* It is interested in votes, in campaign funds, and in patronage. It is governed mainly by fear; therefore it is especially interested in colorable threats of opposition—in other words, blackmail. It is easy to recall how horribly it was harried by the lash of the Anti-Saloon League, and we are now seeing it kept awake nights by dread of the Townsendites, Sinclairites, Olsonites, La Folletteites, share-the-wealthers, and other irreconcilables. Therefore the seekers after State intervention must propose satisfactory terms of brokerage in one or another of the foregoing ways, and if they are able to do so, the intervention is forthcoming.

The employment of this technique brings about a condition that invites unscrupulous exploitation. Consequently, whenever the State makes a positive intervention, it is at once urged to make another one to regulate or supervise this exploitation in behalf of persons or groups which are unfavorably affected. This second intervention is found in turn to be exploitable, interested persons proceed to exploit it, and the State makes another intervention at the request of influential groups who are being squeezed. Then further exploitation, another intervention, then another and so on indefinitely, pyramiding set after set of exploitable complications, until the whole structure falls to pieces at a touch, as our banking structure did three years ago. I was interested to see that the new banking bill proposed last summer by the Senate covered almost four pages of the *Wall Street Journal!* If the State had never made any positive interventions upon the banking business or any other business, a perfectly competent banking law could be set up in ten lines, non-pareil. The action of the State in trying to check exploitation of one positive intervention by making another and another in a series of ever-increasing particularity, is like the action of a horse that has stepped in quicksand—each succeeding step only sinks him deeper.

The State, however, is always glad to take advantage of these collisions of interest, because each positive intervention widens the scope of its own jurisdiction, enhances its prestige, and adds to its accumulation of power. It cuts down the individual's margin of action, and pushes up the State's margin. These gains are all made at the expense of society, so it may be said that, in the social view, the State's positive interventions are a mechanism for converting social power into State power; the reason being that there is no other source from which State power can be drawn. All the power the State has is what society gives it, or what under one pretext or another it confiscates from society; and all the power thus transferred which is spent on expanding and maintaining the State's structure is just so much out of what society can apply to its own purposes.

This can be illustrated in terms of money. There seems to be an impression in some quarters that the State has money of its own. It has none. All the money it has is what it takes from society, and society gets money by the production of wealth; that is, by applying labor and capital to natural resources. There is no other way to produce wealth than this, and hence there is no source but production from which money can be got. All the money that the State takes by way of taxes, therefore, must come out of production for there is no other place for it to come from. All it takes, then, leaves society with that much less to go on with.

The same thing is true with regard to the rest of society's resources. We all know that certain virtues and integrities are the root of stability. Wealth has relatively little to do with keeping society's head above water; the character and spirit of the people is what does it. Every positive intervention of the State tends to reduce the margin of existence which the individual is free to regulate for himself; and to the extent to which it does reduce it, it is a levy on character. Independence of mind, self-respect, dignity, self-reliance–such virtues are the real and great resources of society, and every confiscation of them by the State leaves society just so much poorer. For instance, in 1932, when Mr. Roosevelt announced the doctrine that the State owes every citizen a living, the State, under his direction, took advantage of an unusual contingency to bring about a wholesale conversion of social power into State power. As we all know, it made a prodigious levy on social money-power, but that is relatively a small matter. Society will never get it back–the machine-crew, operating under whatever political label, will see to that–but further levies may for a time be somewhat checked, though probably very little. What America does not realize is that the intervention of 1932 put a levy on the character of the people which is beyond any estimate and beyond any possible hope of recovery. There are millions of people in the country today who not only believe that the State owes them a living, but who are convinced that they will never get a living unless the State gives it to them. They are so despoiled of the moral resources that alone keep society in vigor that one may say they look to the State to validate every breath they draw.

II

In the foregoing I have tried to show a few of the signs and roadmarks on the way to collectivism, and to give an idea of the distance America has already gone along that way, and also to show what the stimulus is that is driving us continually further. Collectivism means the absorption of *all* social power by the State; it means that the individual lives *for* the State. As an individual, he ceases to exist; he can think of himself, as so many millions of our people now do, as only a creature of the State. The free, intelligent exercise of those virtues and integrities which are the capital resources of society is replaced by a wholly irrational and canine obedience to the minutiae of coercive State control.

Collectivism is the orderly and inevitable upshot of the course we have taken from the beginning. The country is committed to collectivism, not by circumstances, not by accident, not by anything but a progressive degeneration in the spirit and character of a whole people under the corrupting influence of a dominant idea—the idea that government exists to help business. I have already several times said publicly—and I have been much blamed for saying it, when I have not been merely ridiculed—not only that I firmly believe America is headed for out-and-out collectivism, but that the momentum we have gained in a century and a half is now so strong that nothing can be done about it, and certainly nothing can be done about its consequences. In saying this I have been guided only by observing the dominance of this one idea throughout our history, by observing the marked degeneration in character and spirit which I speak of, and by perceiving the natural necessity whereby the one must follow upon the other. It strikes me that any thoughtful American may well and prayerfully take notice of where we have come out on the deal by which we got the thing symbolized by the stars and stripes and *E Pluribus Unum* in exchange for the thing symbolized by the rattlesnake flag of the horse-and-buggy days, with its legend, *Don't Tread On Me.*

An acquaintance said to me the other day that he did not believe the country could stand another four years under Mr. Roosevelt. I said I had no opinion about that; what I was sure of was that no country could stand indefinitely being ruled by the spirit and character of a people who would tolerate Mr. Roosevelt for fifteen minutes, let alone four years. I was of course speaking of the generic Roosevelt; the personal Roosevelt is a mere bit of the *Oberhefe* which specific gravity brings to the top of the Malebolge of politics. He does not count, and his rule does not count. What really counts is the spirit and character of a people willing under any circumstances whatever to accept the genus, whether the individual specimen who offers himself be named Roosevelt, Horthy, Hitler, Mussolini, or Richard Roe.

A republic is adjusted to function at the level of the lowest common denominator of its people. I take it that among many pretty clear indications of where that level stands in America, one is the fact, if it be a fact, that twelve million signatures have been subscribed to petitions for the Townsend Plan. I have only a press report as authority for this, so let us discount it fifty per cent for journalistic enterprise, and say six million.

Here then, apparently, is a good share of the population which not only does not want the government to stop making positive interventions upon the individual, but is urging it to multiply them to an extent hitherto unheard of. Then on the other hand, there is what in the popular scale of speech is called the business world. I can not imagine that there are a baker's dozen in that world who would regard a government that really kept its hands off business–which is what some of them pretend to want–as anything but an appalling calamity, worse than the earthquake of Lisbon. We can almost hear the yells of horror that would go up from every chamber of commerce, bankers' conference, and Rotarian lunch-table, if they were suddenly confronted with a governmental announcement that the policy of positive intervention was henceforth and forever in the discard. Suppose the next President, whoever he may be, should say in his inaugural address: "No more positive interventions of any kind. The Department of Commerce and the Department of Labor will shut up shop tomorrow. No more concern with any form of business except to see that it is run straight, and no more legalism about that, either. Beginning tomorrow, the Department of Justice will cease being a Department of Law, and become a real Department of Justice." Would the business world welcome a statement of policy like that? Hardly. Thus it would appear that the level of the lowest common denominator is in this respect pretty low. In other words, practically no one wants the uniform policy of positive State intervention changed for a uniform policy of purely negative intervention. Each would probably be willing enough to see that policy vacated in the case of all the others; but to see it vacated *for him* is simply something that will not bear thinking about.

Very well, then, the question is, how can America insist upon a policy of taking all the successive steps which lead directly to collectivism, and yet avoid collectivism? I do not see how it can be done. Nor do I see how it is possible to have collectivism and not incur the consequences of collectivism. The vestiges of many civilizations are witness that it has never yet been done, nor is it at all clear how the present civilization can make itself exempt.

Crossing the ocean last year, I struck up an acquaintance with a lawyer from New York. Our talk turned on public affairs, and he presently grew confidential. He said: "I could work five times as hard as I do, and make more than five times the money I do, but why should I? The government would take most of my money away, and the balance would not be enough to pay for the extra work."

One can generalize from this incident, insignificant as it is. The cost of the State's positive interventions has to be paid out of production, and thus they tend to retard production, according to the maxim that the power to tax is the power to destroy. The resulting stringencies, inconveniences, and complications bring about further interventions which still further depress production; and these sequences are repeated until production ceases entirely, as it did at Rome in the third century, when there was simply not enough production to pay the State's bills.

I repeat that I can see no better prospect than this as long as the tendency to collectivism goes on unchecked, and as I have shown, there seems to be no discoverable disposition to check it–the prevailing spirit and character of the people, on the contrary, seem all in its favor. Well then, I should say agreement must be made with the conclusion of Professor Ortega y Gasset, that "the result of this tendency will be fatal. Spontaneous social action will be broken up over and over again by State intervention; no new seed will be able to fructify. Society will have to live *for* the State, men *for* the governmental machine. And as after all it is only a machine, whose existence and maintenance depend on the vital supports around it, the State, after sucking out the very marrow of society, will be left bloodless, a skeleton, dead with the rusty death of machinery, more gruesome than the death of a living organism. Such was the lamentable fate of ancient civilization."

7
PIECEMEAL COLLECTIVISM
Walter Lippmann*

Walter Lippmann's career as social critic has spanned the era from the First World War to the war in Vietnam. A socialist when he left Harvard in 1910, Lippmann had by 1914 become an ardent advocate of progressive reform. Yet while his *Drift and Mastery* (1914) remains one of the most influential statements of the progressive position, the debacle of the war and the League of Nations controversy caused Lippmann to abandon progressivism much as he had earlier rejected socialism. During the 1920's Lippmann sought to understand the relationship between public opinion and democracy. He concluded, in *Public Opinion* (1922), that a governmental system that presupposed the existence of an informed, rational public made little sense, for men ordinarily mistook images for reality and were influenced by organized pressure groups. Having come full circle by the 1930's, Lippmann emerged as a chief critic of the Roosevelt administration. In *The Good Society* (1937), Lippmann objected to the collectivist order because it tended to "obscure and distort the whole moral conception of income as the reward of useful work, or poverty as the punishment for laziness and imprudence"; this was properly regarded as an assault on the New Deal. Yet his own program bore a striking resemblance to Roosevelt's. Lippmann favored "large social expenditures on eugenics and on education," conservation, public works projects to reclaim land and develop water power, and "insurance and indemnification against the risks and losses of technological and economic change." All of this would be financed by graduated taxes, especially on unearned incomes and monopoly profits. It is in this context that Lippmann's article, with its harsh denunciation of bureaucratic government and its argument that democratic control and economic planning were incompatible, should be read. □

---

*Lippmann, Walter, Piecemeal Collectivism, *The Atlantic Monthly,* **CLIX** (February, 1937), 228-38. Reprinted by permission of Walter Lippmann.

In countries like Great Britain or the United States there is no manifest disposition to establish a totalitarian order with a regimented population under a militarized autocracy, but for some sixty years these democracies have tended increasingly to seek relief from poverty and disorder by the use of collectivist measures. In fact it may be said that contemporary progressives are gradual collectivists and that they hope by the gradualness of their methods to establish a collectivist order piecemeal, and thus avoid the violence of dictatorship.

Those who hold this view are at present the overwhelming majority of public-spirited and well-disposed persons in the democratic countries. They are not fanatics who, in order to achieve a planned society, would be willing to sweep away the guaranties of liberty and the responsibility of rulers to the people. Their goal is the public administration of the economy, but they believe that no step must be taken to that goal without popular consent obtained by persuasion in open debate. They hold that in this way the advance into collectivism can be made without class struggle, dictatorship, or the militarization of society.

For approximately three generations a gradual democratic advance into collectivism has been under way. This movement also has its ideology. But here again, as with the fascists and the communists, theory is very unlike practice and the results are very different from the promises.

THE THEORY

The theory of gradual collectivism rests upon the assumption that majorities express the will and represent the interests of society, and that they have inherited from the king the prerogatives of sovereignty. The gradual collectivist believes in the absolutism of the majority, having by a fiction identified the mandates of transient majorities with the enduring and diverse purposes of the members of a community. He thinks it absurd that a few oligarchs in the Kremlin or demagogic dictators in Berlin or Rome should pretend that their personal decisions are the comprehensive purposes of great nations. Yet the gradual collectivist, under the banner of popular sovereignty, believes in the dictatorship of random aggregations of voters. In this theory the individual has no rights as against the majority—constitutional checks and bills of rights exist only by consent of the majority. Even the right of the majority to rule is at the mercy of any passing majority. There is nothing in the doctrine of the sovereignty of the majority to preclude the abolition of majority rule by vote of a majority.

In fact it was under the aegis of this doctrine that Napoleon III and Hitler came to power.

Thus by one fiction the gradual collectivist identifies passing majorities with the nation. By another fiction he treats the legislators as representative of the majorities which elected them. And finally, by a third fiction he pretends that the executive and administrative machine represents the wills of a majority of the legislators. The nation is supposed to have delegated its unlimited authority to a majority of the enfranchised voters. They are supposed to have delegated their unlimited authority to a majority in the legislative assembly. The assembly is supposed to have delegated its unlimited authority to the executive and the bureaucracy. To this central authority the gradual collectivist then proposed to entrust increasingly the administration of the social system.

It is evident that a régime of this sort is afflicted with an insoluble contradiction. In so far as it seeks to administer the economy under a rational and coherent plan, it must somehow prevent one majority from overriding the decisions of a previous majority. For if a plan is to be carried out, it must be adopted and the people must thereafter conform. If they do not conform, if they are free at any time to agitate for amendments, the plan ceases to be a plan. It would not be a plan if its parts were not closely interrelated; if it is subject to continual change at vital points, the whole design has to be remade continually. Suppose, for example, that the Russian people had had democratic control over the Five-Year Plan, and that, having assented at the outset to the proposal that they should manufacture steel before they manufactured clothing, they had changed their minds. In making this change they would not have amended the plan: they would have abolished it. It would then have been necessary to draft a wholly different plan, and two years after the new plan had been put into effect the people might again have changed their minds. This would have called for still a different plan. But a series of different plans is no plan at all.

The very essence of the democratic process is that the rulers are continually responsible to popular opinion, and unless that opinion is free to change, and in changing to alter the policy of the state, there is no democracy. The very essence of the conception of planning is that a design can be adopted to which the people will thereafter conform. This is equivalent to saying that a democratic people cannot have a planned economy, and that in so far as they desire planned economy they must suspend responsible government.

THE POLITY OF PRESSURE GROUPS

In the real world the historic advance of democratic collectivism has not been directed by the rationalized vision of a new society. It is true these visions have influenced the argument over specific measures, rousing many to action and breaking down resistance, and it would be difficult to exaggerate the practical influence on western society of these collectivists who call themselves social democrats, Fabian socialists, evolutionary or revisionist socialists, or merely progressives. The collectivists have conquered the intellectual world, to borrow a phrase from Mr. Keynes, as thoroughly as the Holy Inquisition conquered Spain. They have made it seem rather ridiculous and contemptible to hold that mankind can advance by proceeding with the process of liberation; they have persuaded the intellectual world that social improvement must come by magnifying the dominion of the state. But though collectivists exercise a kind of intellectual monopoly and absolute authority over the assumptions of modern political thought, they have not imbued the mass of the people with their own general conception of society as a whole. The doctrines remain the possession of an élite. Electorates and parliaments, though they have been moving rapidly in the collectivist direction, have not consciously been shaping society according to a new design.

Though the movement has been under way for more than sixty years, up to the present time no socialist party in any of the large western democracies has obtained the support of an effective majority of the electorate. It is a matter of common knowledge that even when the socialist vote has been considerable it is no measure of the number of genuinely convinced and indoctrinated socialists. There are many more socialist voters than there are convinced socialists. Thus it is fair to say that the advance of collectivism has not been determined by the image of a collectivist society. The advance has consisted of a series of definite measures, all more or less within the same general category, to be sure. But these measures have come not from a general theory but from a series of efforts to deal with specific grievances and to provide particular benefits.

Such has been the inner principle of the gradual and democratic collectivist movement. It is, I believe, its only possible principle. Because a democracy cannot adopt a collectivist plan, the practical initiative in each measure of its gradual advance comes not from the energy of a general ideal but from organized interests seeking protection and privileges. In practice, gradual collectivism is not an ordered scheme of social reconstruction. It is the polity of pressure groups.

The movement advances by measures adopted from time to time at the instigation of aggrieved or aspiring groups of voters. Through their leaders and lobbyists they persuade, cajole, coerce, and occasionally corrupt the electorate or the parliament; often they conspire with other organized interests to form majorities by coalition. Though exceptions could be cited, it is substantially true that, while the moral and intellectual justification for each measure is derived from the general ideology of collectivism, the initiative comes from organized interests. There has been some legislation for the welfare of the weak and the dependent which may be said to be the work of humane and disinterested men. But these measures do not deeply affect the conduct of business and government. Though they are humanly important, they are peripheral and superficial, and by all thoroughgoing collectivists are recognized as such.

The measures which have profoundly affected the social order because they have meant the shift of important social benefits from one group to another, from one region or occupation to another, from individuals to great corporations, or from individuals to the government—all such decisive measures have proceeded from the pressure of interested groups upon the electorate and upon the politicians. The particular measures would not have been adopted when they were adopted but for the organized agitation, the lobbying, and the exercise of influence by these interested groups. Thus no serious historian of politics would imagine that he had accounted for the protective tariff or the system of bounties or subsidies, for the monetary and the banking laws, for the state of the law in regard to corporate privileges and immunities, for the actual status of property rights, for agricultural or for labor policies, until he had gone behind the general claims and the abstract justifications and had identified the specifically interested groups which promoted the specific law.

Such an understanding of the actual history should not be confused with the arbitrary classification of society into a capitalist class and a proletarian class. For while it may serve the purposes of a revolutionary propaganda to say with Marx that the modern state is 'nothing more than a committee for the administration of the consolidated affairs of the bourgeois class as a whole,' the specific measures taken by modern states are unintelligible on the hypothesis that there is a 'bourgeois class' which has 'consolidated affairs.' Consider, for example, the American tariff as it existed when President Hoover signed the Hawley-Smoot bill in 1930. It would be admitted by all, I suppose, that with negligible exceptions each item in each schedule originated with at least some of the producers of the commodity protected by the duty, and that the rate was either a grant of their demands or a compromise between their demands and the objections raised by representatives of some other interest. No one would pretend that this tariff which profoundly affected the whole American economy, not to speak of the economy of the world, was in any sense of the term conceived by the 'bourgeois class' as a whole. The very essence of that tariff, and of all its predecessors, was that, far from representing the 'consolidated' interests of business men as a class, it represented the special interests of some of them.

Under gradual collectivism, precisely because it is gradual, the measures of state interference are almost invariably promoted by particular groups. Invariably they claim that their particular interest is identical with the national interest. But it is the particular interest which moves them to raise the issue. The legislature may reject the claim if someone is able to expose its fallacy. But in so far as the legislature acts, it must listen to some petition. It does not move unless it has been provoked by the claim of some group. For it has no other criterion by means of which it can decide where and when and to what end it should intervene.

Particularity, both of origin and of incidence, is the essence of the specific measures whereby gradual collectivism develops. The protective tariff does not stand alone. The same principle is no less evident in the collectivist measures designed to assist farmers or workers. The very fact that they are generally proposed on the ground that something must be done to equalize burdens, privileges, and bargaining power is in itself a most significant indication of the real nature of the process. If we examine such measures in detail we shall rarely fail to observe that in fact they are promoted not by 'the farmers' or by 'labor' as a whole but by particular interests among farmers and workingmen.

The Agricultural Adjustment Act, for example, in its dealings with cotton, paid little attention to the tenant farmers, the share-croppers, not to speak of the agricultural laborers who were displaced by the curtailment of cotton production. Moreover, the curtailment of cotton production by the method of acreage reduction paid scant attention to the claims of the efficient producer as against those of the less efficient. Furthermore, the act itself selected nine 'basic' commodities which were entitled to benefit payments. All the other farmers had to contribute to these benefits by paying the processing taxes. Thus a dairyman paid a tax on cotton, wheat, hogs, and corn, but received no benefit payments. I do not mean to argue that, in the critical conditions which prevailed in the year 1933, special legislation of this sort may not have been temporarily in the general interest. My concern is merely to illustrate the underlying principle of gradual collectivism, which is that its specific measures owe their origin to particular interests and that its design follows the pattern of the influences exerted by pressure groups.

The same principle tends to control labor legislation. Anyone who will analyze the laws passed to benefit labor will find that, apart from some few of a humanitarian character, they reflect with fair accuracy the strategic advantages of certain groups of workers. Thus railroad employees are more highly protected by special laws than any other group, and among railroad employees the members of the brotherhoods are more carefully protected than the shopmen or the unskilled workers who maintain the tracks. The social security laws providing for insurance against unemployment, for example, and the laws to promote collective bargaining give protection to well-established, strategically placed, and highly organized groups. They are quite unable to give the same degree of protection, let us say, to domestic servants, to clerks, or to casual workers.

THE VICIOUS PARADOX IN THE POLITY OF PRESSURE GROUPS

It appears to make no difference where collectivism of this sort begins. Whether it begins with tariffs for some manufacturers, special laws for certain groups of workingmen, or bounties for farmers, the one certain thing is that in a democratic society the granting of some privileges must be followed by the granting of more privileges. In fact it might be said that when modern states abandoned the Jeffersonian principle of special privileges to none they became committed, by the sentiment for equal rights, to the principle of special privileges for all.

Thus a tariff for one industry will make irresistible the demands of other industries for equal protection. At the end of the process, very nearly reached by the United States in 1930, tariffs become universal and well-nigh exclusive against all foreign products that can be made domestically. But such tariffs only mark the beginning. The agricultural interests will demand protection and bounties in order to achieve 'parity.' An advanced system of labor legislation always demands the support of an exclusive tariff. Thus under the National Industrial Recovery Act, which sought by federal laws, called codes, to elevate wages and working conditions, it was provided that if 'substantial quantities' of any article were imported, and might 'render ineffective' the 'maintenance of any code,' such imports could be prohibited.

Now the effect of attempting to give protection to all the interests capable of bringing influence to bear upon the government is to cancel many of their special advantages. One tariff-protected manufacturer in an economy otherwise committed to free trade will, of course, obtain a substantial advantage. But, if the producer from whom he buys his raw materials is also given protection, some of that benefit is canceled, for the costs of production are increased. If, then, bounties and tariffs have to be given to the farmers in order to protect them also, the first lobbyist not only has to contribute to the benefits out of his profits, but finds that the cost of living has risen for his employees. When they organize to increase their real wages, more of his benefits are canceled.

If the sole effect of this cumulative collectivism were to cancel the special advantages of the various pressure groups, it might be regarded as a harmless method of letting them enjoy the appearance of special privileges while the community escaped the consequences. If, by making privilege universal, special advantages were neutralized; if, by giving one interest after another a special favor, all the interests came to be on an equal footing, the process might be silly, but it would not be dangerous. The believers in gradual collectivism seem to have some such comforting thought in the backs of their minds.

The notion of equal privileges for every interest has, as it happens, been elaborated into a scheme of social organization. It is known in Italy as the Corporative State. In Russia it is partially embodied in the Soviet system of government. And long before that the idea was adopted by several schools of social reconstruction, among them the guild socialists and syndicalists of many sorts.

The theory of these schemes is that government should be 'functional' rather than geographical—that is to say, in the state each person should be represented as a worker rather than as a citizen. Many democrats have been attracted by the idea, thinking that the avowed representation of particular interests would be better than the lobbying of pressure groups pretending to be disinterested patriots. They have been tempted to hope that the open avowal of all special interests would neutralize their self-regarding purposes into a realistic but harmonious conception of the general interest. The trouble with the scheme is that it sanctifies the self-regarding purposes of special interests and does nothing to subdue them. For many particular interests do not in any conceivable combination constitute the general interest; to entrust the government of a nation to such a body would be to turn the sovereign power over to a coalition of its most powerful interests. As a matter of fact, though the semblance of such a political organization exists in Italy, in Russia, and even in Germany, no real power is entrusted to it in any of these states. The sovereign power resides in the dictatorship, and in fact only a dictatorship could hope to keep a chamber of special interests from conspiring continually against the national welfare.

There is no reason to think that the self-regarding activities of special groups can be compensated or regulated by organizing more and more of them. In the historical period during which organized interests have been increasingly active and their activities treated as more and more reputable, there have been two momentous developments. By organized restrictions of many sorts the production of wealth has been retarded, the method of monopoly being employed to enrich the favored interests. The imprimatur of respectability having been put upon organized privilege, the whole population has become imbued with the idea that as a matter of right everyone is entitled to invoke the law to increase his income.

This is the vicious paradox of the gradual collectivism which has developed in western society during the past sixty years: it has provoked the *expectation* of universal plenty provided by action of the state while, through almost every action undertaken or tolerated by the state, the production of wealth is *restricted.* By these measures modern states have frustrated the hopes which their policies have aroused. They have put into effect measures of scarcity, and all the while they have taught the people that the effect of the policy would be to give them abundance. To that paradox no small part of the dangerous tension in modern society is due.

THE RESTRICTION OF WEALTH

That a system of gradual collectivism, operating through tariffs and bounties, price fixing and wage fixing, must reduce the wealth of nations has seemed so self-evident to a long line of economists that one of them has been moved to say that 'only the feeble-minded and the paid agents of vested interests will be found to deny such propositions' (Lionel Robbins, in *The Great Depression*). Yet the proposition is denied in the practice of all modern states, and among the great mass of their inhabitants it is regarded as far from self-evident that to restrict production is to become deliberately poorer.

It is curious and significant, however, that while almost every interest favors collectivist measures, no one defends them all. Thus, for example, the processing tax on cotton–levied in order to pay cotton planters to restrict their output and raise the price–was invalidated in the Supreme Court as the result of a lawsuit brought by a textile mill corporation which enjoys high tariff protection. Manufacturers, who have the legal privilege of exclusive possession of the domestic market at more than a competitive price, have no difficulty in understanding the objections to laws which create artificially high prices for their raw materials. They can see no less easily the fallacy of monopolistic union wage rates. All the reasons for respecting the law of supply and demand, all the arguments against monopoly, restriction, and scarcity, are self-evident to them except in the field where they themselves have an exclusive market under government protection.

The managers of the great corporations are fully aware that the production of wealth is restricted by labor laws and labor contracts which enable their employees to do less work for more pay. But it is not so easy for them to see that when, by means of tariffs or a monopolistic control of prices, they restrict production and raise their prices above the competitive level they too are practising a policy of scarcity. Though they will shut down their own plant rather than sell at a lower price, and will invoke tariff protection to prevent foreigners from selling at the lower price, they nevertheless understand that the soundest principles of economics have been violated when farmers are assisted by the government to plough under cotton and slaughter little pigs, when wage earners insist on shorter hours at a high 'prevailing wage.' These same farmers, however, relying upon the full power of the government to raise their prices by restricting production, will in the same breath denounce the railroads and utilities for not expanding production by reducing the rates.[1]

Thus, in the debate which accompanies the advance of gradual collectivism, particular interests will be found advocating protection for themselves and free trade for those with whom they transact their affairs. If the student is looking for a defense of the system, he can find it by assembling the arguments used by each interest in defending its special privilege. But an equally impressive collection of separate briefs could be assembled, written by spokesmen for the same interests, denouncing as uneconomic, as immoral, as unconstitutional, often as treasonable and subversive, the same practices when carried on by other interests.

---

[1]Compare, for example, the price policy of the Tennessee Valley Authority, which has the backing of the farm bloc, with that of the Agricultural Adjustment Administration.–Author

These self-contradictory pleadings are such glaring instances of man's ability to see the mote in his neighbor's eye and to overlook the beam in his own that one is led to ask how the disinterested exponents of gradual collectivism can persuade themselves that they have a rational political philosophy. At the level of practical politics there are the pulling and pushing of interested groups contending for the assistance of the sovereign power. At the level of popular debate there are the special pleas of interests, each insisting that the general interest will be served if the coercive authority of the state is placed at its disposal. The gradual collectivist has to suppose that over and above these special groups and their special pleadings there exists a sovereign power able to discern the universal in the particular, and to assert it with the force of law. He has to suppose that the electorate and its parliament have a criterion, presumably a body of principles, by which, after they have felt all the pressures and heard all the arguments, they can determine which imports to restrict, which industries and regions and occupations to favor, which prices and wages to fix and at what rate to fix them.

It is important that we make clear to ourselves the real character of the judgments which the method of gradual collectivism requires the voters and their representatives to make. They are not expected merely to interpret and enforce a system of established rights among vested interests. On the contrary, they are asked to create a series of new rights, some to replace old ones, most of them, however, in addition to the old ones. Thus they destroy some vested rights and call into being others. The arbitrament required of a democracy under gradual collectivism is, therefore, a peculiarly difficult one. It calls for the continual creation of new special privileges; it has to be assumed that the people and their parliaments can judge correctly which special privileges will be, and which will not be, for the general welfare. For under gradual collectivism the state does not merely enforce existing rights. Nor does it repeal privileges and liquidate vested interests. It establishes partnerships in more and more fields between the government and certain selected interests. The government has, therefore, to decide continually with which interests it will go into partnership and on what terms.

The real nature of gradual collectivism was made extraordinarily clear in the New Deal, as it existed before the Supreme Court of the United States invalidated it. Under the National Industrial Recovery Act, industries were encouraged to organize themselves as agents of the state. To each of these groups there was then delegated the power to legislate not only for all who were then engaged in that line of business but for all who might wish to engage in it. No clearer, no more naked, illustration could be offered of what is meant by the statement that gradual collectivism means the conferring of privileges upon selected interests. For the right to make laws and to enforce them by fines and imprisonment is the basic attribute of sovereignty, and the delegation of sovereignty to selected interests is exactly what the word 'privilege' means. In the case of the NRA, privilege was conferred upon certain trade organizations and theoretically at least upon industrial employees also. The industrial codes were in effect charters–like those once granted to the East India Company, like those now granted to municipal corporations–to exercise the sovereign power within a certain jurisdiction.

Under the Agricultural Adjustment Act, and under such ancillary laws as the Bankhead Cotton and the Kerr Tobacco Act, the conferring of privilege and the delegation of the state's authority to particular groups were not quite so nakedly evident. Nevertheless, that was the essence of the matter. Out of all the farmers of America and among all the crops they produce, Congress selected eight staples, and authorized the Secretary of Agriculture to levy taxes and to apply the proceeds in a subsidy to the producers of those eight staples. The producers of these selected commodities were established as a vested interest, protected by laws and by a subsidy in their right to produce their crop as against anyone who might wish to trespass upon their right to produce and sell cotton. It is significant that the established growers of the basic commodities were not only given a privileged position as against all other farmers, but that among them the cotton and tobacco growers had a specially favored position. Whether that was due to the fact that cotton and tobacco were peculiarly hard hit, or to the fact that they occupy a strategic position in the political composition of the Democratic Party, is perhaps a matter of opinion. But it is undeniably clear that the privileges were conferred approximately in proportion to the influence of particular pressure groups.

The gradual collectivist has to believe that a mass of special privileges can be distributed among interested groups in such a way as to raise the general standard of life. He has to believe that an elected parliament will distribute its privileges according to some general conception of the public welfare and not according to the pull and push of organized interests. Is this conceivable in a democracy? It is conceivable, of course, under a dictatorship if it be granted that the dictator knows in general and in particular what is for the public welfare. It does not seem likely that an electorate, listening to the babel of special pleadings, would be able to detect the universal interest in the particular, except occasionally and by good luck. There is, as Professor Carver has said, 'at least a theoretical possibility for improvement through restrictive regulation. A system of privileges is imaginable which would be so nicely designed and so delicately adjusted that it would raise the standard of life by increasing the production of wealth and improving its distribution.' But no economist has ever designed such a system and the chances are small that a democracy could see through the special pleadings, would be able to resist the pressures, and could know even with approximate accuracy which interests to favor and in what degree. If the experiment could be repeated often enough, under the law of chances a democracy might hit upon the right system of privileges. But so, as an eminent philosopher once remarked, could a band of monkeys who had learned to hit the keys of a typewriter turn out a play of Shakespeare's—if they kept at it through all eternity.

For while a system of privileges *might* theoretically augment wealth, the chances are overwhelming that most of the privileges granted will be reducible to a common denominator. With few exceptions they will be a guarantee, backed by the authority of the state, that the beneficiaries will receive a larger private income for less effort. This means that those who are not beneficiaries will have a smaller income in return for more effort. On the whole and in the ordinary run of human affairs, tariffs, subsidies, regulated prices and wages, are promoted by men seeking to obtain a larger income, not by producing more wealth but by obtaining a larger share of the wealth produced.

Thus, when a tariff duty prevents the domestic consumer from purchasing the most inexpensive steel that can be produced in the world, the state has said that the nation either must use less steel or, if it insists on the same amount of steel, must be content with less goods of other kinds. The capital and labor and managerial skill devoted to making the more expensive steel are no longer available to make other goods. The same principle applies to the regulation of particular prices and particular wages. If they are set high, and are effective, they exact a subsidy from others; if they are set low, the victims are sweated to subsidize others. Those who receive the subsidy obtain more income for less effort; those who pay the subsidy have less income for more effort. But since a system of gradual collectivism will always tend to favor the interests that are organized, are identified, and are insistent, since they will not be insistent because they wish to work harder but only because they wish to receive more by not working harder, the grand effect of the system is to diminish the production of wealth.

RISING EXPECTATIONS

Even if it could not be demonstrated that mankind is poorer because it has embraced collectivism, it is undeniable that the people have been taught by the collectivists to believe that the government can and should make them richer. The farmers and wage earners who come asking for tariffs, bounties, monopoly in their markets, fixed prices for their goods and services, are merely following the example of the manufacturers who told them that protection produces prosperity and that concentrated corporate control produces stability and security. In a society which has adopted the collectivist view, there is a standing invitation to everyone to devise some method by which the authority of the government can be used to improve his income. For that reason the great teacher of collectivism has not been Karl Marx; it has been the example set by the men who, in the course of more than sixty years, have successfully invoked for their own profit the assistance of the state. It is not the socialist propaganda which has converted the nations; it is the practice of gradual collectivism which has caused the people to think that if some can be enriched by the action of the state, then all might be enriched by it.

The older doctrine was that wealth is increased by labor, enterprise, and thrift, and that the way to a just distribution of income is through the repeal of privileges. It has been overwhelmed by the practical demonstration that some men prosper greatly when the government assists them. So the people have had it fixed in their minds that the state possesses a magical power to provide an abundant life. They have come gradually to think that their expectations may be as great as their government is powerful; that the stronger the government, the more certainly it can satisfy their heart's desires. After a while, when the doctrine is completely dominant in the popular mind, a point is reached where men cease to feel that there is any vital connection between production and consumption, between work and wealth. They believe instead that the vital connection is between wealth and the power of the state. It is no longer labor but the law, the force of the state, the might of the government, that is looked upon as the source of material well-being.

The belief in this miracle is due to an optical illusion. The power of the state, as such, produces nothing: it can only redistribute that which has been produced. Even if the state runs a farm as in Russia or a hydroelectric plant as at Muscle Shoals, the wealth created comes not from the government's power to command and coerce, forbid and defend, but from labor, invention, and the resources of nature. The reason why the state *appears* by exercising power to create wealth is that it can enrich some members of the community.

It is an old illusion. On the River Rhine, the most important trade route of Central Europe, there were, in the twelfth century, nineteen stations at which tolls had to be paid. They were collected by armed forces from the castles whose ruins still delight the tourist. Twenty-five more tolls were added in the thirteenth century, and by the end of the fourteenth century their number had grown to approximately sixty-two or sixty-four.

Many of these stations belonged to the Duchy of Cleves and they were known as the 'treasure.' Now these tolls added nothing, of course, to the wealth of Europe, but they greatly enriched those who took the tolls. In this example, which is typical of all privileges, political force did not produce the 'treasure.' It exacted treasure from those who had produced it. The optical illusion arises because men mistake for the production of wealth the enrichment of those who take the tolls.

The popular belief in the efficacy of the state has its empirical support in the fact that under various forms of protection and privilege, such as tariffs, bounties, franchises, patent monopolies, concentrated corporate control, many have undoubtedly been enriched. If they, why not others? Thus the unprivileged come forward demanding privileges too—privileges to compensate them, to give them parity with, to give them equality of bargaining power with, to give them protection from, those who enjoy the favors that the state bestows. For the inner principle of gradual collectivism—and its radical fallacy—is that it does not dismantle the castles on the Rhine and abolish the privileged toll stations; it attempts—vainly—to turn every cottage into a castle with a toll station of its own.

THE STRUGGLE FOR POWER

Thus it has come about that under gradual collectivism the struggle for power has become ever more intense. As men learn that their fortunes depend increasingly upon their political position, the control of the authority of the state becomes a prize of infinite value. But because the multiplication of the privileges restricts the production of wealth and perverts its distribution, the standard of living does not rise in proportion to the expectations which have been aroused by the example of those who are enriched by privileges. Thus, as gradual collectivism advances, the competitive struggle for privileges is exacerbated, and it culminates in the condition now prevailing where the internal conflict is transformed into an international conflict for the redistribution of national power and privilege throughout the world.

PART THREE
THE RADICAL PERSPECTIVE

8
REPLIES TO GENERAL JOHNSON
Huey Long* and Charles E. Coughlin†

Both the Reverend Charles E. Coughlin, the "Radio Priest" whose sermons attracted millions of listeners each week, and Huey Long, who controlled Louisiana politics with an iron hand, supported Franklin Roosevelt during his first year in office. By 1935, however, Long had broken with the President for good, and Coughlin was in the process of doing so. Their philosophies appealed to those who had benefited disappointingly little from the First New Deal: Coughlin's to the urban working classes and Long's to impoverished rural dwellers in the South. Both men attacked the administration because they considered it too conservative, and because they themselves hungered for power and influence. By the spring of 1935 Coughlin's National Union for Social Justice was emerging as a rallying point for anti-New Deal sentiment, and Long was being touted as a potential third-party presidential candidate. In March of that year General Hugh S. Johnson, former head of the National Recovery Administration, delivered an address in which he denounced the two as "Pied Pipers." Johnson asserted that while Roosevelt had saved the nation from collapse, the New Deal was faltering because it no longer commanded the "spontaneous cooperation" of the people. This Johnson attributed to Coughlin and Long, who, by preaching pie-in-the-sky doctrines, were deluding the people. Johnson's address was filled with personal invective.

---

*Long, Huey, Our Blundering Government and Its Spokesman, *Vital Speeches,* I (March 25, 1935), 391-97. † Coughlin, Rev. Charles E., A Reply to General Johnson, *Vital Speeches,* I (March 25, 1935), 386-91. Reprinted by permission of *Vital Speeches of the Day.*

He accused Coughlin of profiting from silver speculation and "using the cloak of religion to seek political power." In Louisiana, he added, "Huey is dictator by force of arms and Adolf Hitler has nothing on him any way you care to look at them both." Since the radio networks carried Johnson's speech, they granted Long and Coughlin time to reply. Both took the opportunity to present their plans for economic revival in some detail. □

SENATOR HUEY LONG

Ladies and Gentlemen: It has been publicly announced that the White House orders of the Roosevelt administration have declared a war.

The lately lamented, pampered ex-Crown Prince, General Hugh S. Johnson, one of those satelites loaned by Wall Street to run the government, and who at the end of his control over and dismissal from the ill-fated NRA pronounced it as a dead do-do—this Mr. Johnson was apparently selected to make the lead-off speech in this White House charge begun on last Monday night.

The Johnson speech was followed by a fluster and flurry on behalf of the administration by spellbinders in and out of Congress. In a far-away island when a queen dies her first favorite is done the honor to be buried with her.

The funeral procession of the NRA, another one of these New Deal schisms and isms, is about ready to take place. It is said that General Johnson's speech of Monday night to attack me was delivered on the eve of announcing the publication of his own obituary in the Red Book Magazine.

It seems, then, that soon this erstwhile deranged alphabet makes ready to appear at the funeral of NRA, likened to the colored lady in Mississippi who, at such a funeral, asserted, "I is the wife of these remains."

I shall undertake to cover my main subject and make answer to these gentlemen in the course of this speech. It will serve no useful purpose to our distressed people for me to call my opponents more bitter names than they called me. Even were I able, I have not the time to present my side of the argument and match them in profanity.

What is the trouble with this administration of Mr. Roosevelt and of Mr. Johnson, Mr. Farley, Mr. Astor and all their spoilers and spellbinders?

They think that Huey Long is the cause of all their worry. They go gunning for me, but am I the cause of their misery? Well, they are like old

David Crockett, who went out to hunt a possum. He saw there in the gleam of the moonlight, a possum in the top of the tree, going from limb to limb, so he shot, but he missed. He looked again and he saw the possum. He fired a second time and missed again. Soon he discovered that it was not a possum that he saw at all in the top of that tree; it was a louse in his own eyebrow.

I do not make this illustration to do discredit to any of these distinguished gentlemen: I make it to show how often some of us imagine that we see great trouble being done to us by some one at a distance, when in reality all it may be is a fault in our own make-up. And so is this the case of Mr. Roosevelt or Mr. Farley or Mr. Johnson and of others undertaking to derange the situation today.

The trouble with the Roosevelt administration is that when their schemes and isms have failed, these things I told them not to do, and voted not to do, that they think it will help them to light out on those of us who warned them in the beginning that the tangled messes and experiments would not work.

The Roosevelt administration has had its way for two years. They have been allowed to set up or knock down anything and everybody. There was one difference between Roosevelt and Hoover. Hoover could not get the Congress to carry out the schemes he wanted to try, because we managed to lick him on a roll call in the United States Senate time after time when he had both the Democratic leaders and the Republican leaders trying to put them over.

But it is different with Mr. Roosevelt. He got his plans through Congress, but on cold analysis, they were found to be the same things Hoover tried to pass and failed the year before.

The kitchen Cabinet that sat in to advise Hoover was not different from the kitchen Cabinet which advises Roosevelt. Many of the persons are the same. Many more of those in Roosevelt's kitchen Cabinet are of the same men or set of men who furnished employes to sit in the kitchen Cabinet to advise Mr. Hoover.

Maybe you see a little change in the men waiting on the tables in the dining room, but back in the kitchen, the same set of old cooks are back there fixing up the vittles and the grub for us that cooked up that mess under Hoover. There has never even been a change in the seasoning.

Now do you think this Roosevelt plan for plowing up cotton, corn and wheat, and for pouring milk in the river and for destroying and burying the hogs and cattle by the millions, all while the people starve to death and go naked, do you think these plans were the original ideas of Roosevelt administration?

If you do, you are wrong. The whole idea of that kind of thing first came from Hoover's administration. Don't you remember when Mr. Hoover proposed to plow up every fourth row of cotton? We laughed at him to scorn, and so we beat Mr. Hoover on his plan, but when Mr. Roosevelt started on his plan, it was not to plow up every fourth row of cotton, it was to plow up every third row of cotton. He went Mr. Hoover one-twelfth better.

So it has been, while millions have starved and gone naked and while babies have cried and died wanting milk; so it has been while people begged for meat and bread to eat. Mr. Roosevelt's administration has sailed merrily along, plowing under and destroying the things to eat and wear, with tear-dimmed eyes and hungry souls made to chant for this New Deal so that even their starvation dole is not taken away from them, and meanwhile the food and clothes craved by humanity for their bodies and souls go to destruction and ruin.

What do you call it? Is it government? Maybe so. It looks more like the St. Vitus dance to me.

Now since they have sallied forth with General Johnson to start this holy war on me, let us take a look at this NRA they opened up around here about two years ago. They had parades and Fascist signs, just like Hitler and Mussolini. They started the dictatorship to regiment business and labor much more than any known in Germany and Italy.

The only difference was in the sign. Mussolini's sign for a Fascist was a black shirt. Germany's sign of the Fascist was a swastika. So in America they sidetracked the Stars and Stripes, and the sign of the Blue Eagle was used instead for the NRA.

They proceeded with the NRA. Everything from a peanut stand to a powerhouse had to have a separate book of rules and laws to regulate what they did. If the peanut stand started to sell a sack of goobers, they had to be careful to go through the rule book. One slip of the man and he went to jail.

One fellow pressed a pair of pants and went to jail because he charged 5 cents less than the price set up in the rule book. So they wrote their NRA rule books, code laws and so forth, and got up over 900.

One would be as thick as an unabridged dictionary and as confused as the study of the stars. It would take forty lawyers to tell a shoe shiner merchant how to operate and be sure he didn't go to jail. Some people come to me for advice as a lawyer on trying to run their business. I took several days and couldn't understand it myself. The only thing I could tell them was it couldn't be much worse in jail than it was out of jail with that kind of thing going on in the country, and so to go on and do the best they could.

The whole thing of Mr. Roosevelt as run under General Johnson became such a national scandal that Roosevelt had to let Johnson slide out as a scapegoat. I am told that the day the general had to go, when they had waited just as long as they would wait on him, he wanted to issue a blistering statement against Mr. Roosevelt, but they finally saddled him off because they didn't know but what Wall Street might want to lend him to some other President in the future, so he left without.

It was under this NRA and the other funny alphabetical combinations that followed it that we ran the whole country into a mare's nest. The Farleys and Johnsons combed the land with agents, inspectors, supervisors, detectives, secretaries, assistants, and so forth, all of them armed with the power to arrest anybody and send them to jail if they found them not living up to some one of the rules in these 900 catalogues they had out.

One man, whose case reached the Supreme Court of the United States, I understand, pleaded guilty because he didn't know what it was about, and when it got to the United States Supreme Court, it was turned loose because they couldn't even find a rule book he was supposed to be guided by.

Now it is with the PWA, WRA, GINS and every other flimsy combination that the country finds its affairs in business where no one can recognize it. More men are now out of work than ever. The debt of the United States has gone up ten billion more dollars. There is starvation; there is homelessness; there is misery on every hand and corner. But, mind you, in the meantime, Mr. Roosevelt has had his way. He is one man that can't blame any of his troubles on Huey Long. He has had his way.

Down in my part of the country, if any man has the measles he blames that on me; but there is one man that can't blame anything on anybody but himself and that is Mr. Franklin De-La-No Roose-velt.

And now on top of that, they ordered a war on me because nearly four years ago I told Hoover's crowd, it won't do, and because three years ago I told Roosevelt and his crowd, it won't do. In other words, they are in a rage at Huey Long because I have had to say, "I told you so."

I was not overstating the conditions now prevailing in this country. In the own words of these gentlemen, they have confessed all that I now say or ever have said. Mr. Roosevelt, and Mrs. Roosevelt, too, have lately bewailed the fact that food, clothes and shelter have not been provided for the people. Even this General Hugh S. Johnson has said in his speech of this last Monday night that there are 80,000 babies in America who are badly hurt or wrecked by this depression. He, of course, includes us all in that classification of babies.

Mr. Harry Hopkins, who runs the relief work, says the dole roll has risen now to 22,375,000 people, the highest it has ever been. And now what is there for the Roosevelt crowd to do but to admit the facts, and admit further that they are now in their third year making matters worse instead of better.

No one is to blame except them for what is going on when they have had their way, and they couldn't change the thing in two years. It is now worse than ever, and if they haven't been able to do any good in the way they have been going for two years, how can any one expect any good of them for the next two years to come? God save us two more years of the disaster we have had under that gang.

When this condition of distress and suffering among so many of our people began to develop in the Hoover Administration, we knew what was the trouble, and what we would have to do to correct it.

I was one of the first men to say publicly. Mr. Roosevelt followed in my track a few months later, and said the same thing–we said that all of our trouble and woe was due to the fact that too few of our people owned too much of our wealth.

We said that in our land we've too much to eat and too much to wear, and too many houses to live in; too many automobiles to be sold–that the only trouble was that the people suffered in the land of abundance because too few controlled the money and the wealth, and too many people did not have money which would buy the things they needed for life and comfort.

So I said to the people of the United States in my speeches, which I delivered in the United States Senate and over the radio in the early part of 1932, that the only way by which we could restore to reasonable life and comfort was to limit the size of the big men's fortune and guarantee some minimum to the fortune and comfort of the little man's family.

I said then as I have said since that it was inhuman to have goods rot, cotton and wool going to waste, houses empty, and at the same time to have millions of our people starving, our people naked, our people homeless, because they could not buy the things which other men had and for which these other men had no use.

So we convinced Mr. Franklin Delano Roosevelt that it was necessary that he announce and promise to the American people that in the event he were elected President of the United States he would pull down the size of the big man's fortune and guarantee something to every family, enough to do away with all poverty, and to give employment to those who were able to work and an education to the children born into the world.

Mr. Roosevelt made those promises. He made them before he was nominated in the Chicago convention, he made them again before he was elected in November, and he went so far as to remake those promises a day or two after he was inaugurated President of the United States, and I was one authorized to say so, and I thought for a day or two after he took the oath as President that maybe he was going through with his promises.

But no heart has ever been so saddened, no person's ambition was ever so blighted as was mine when I came to the realization that the President of the United States was not going to undertake what he said he would do, and what I knew to be necessary if the people of America were ever saved from calamity and misery. . . .

And so we arrived, and we are still there at the place in abundant America where we have everything for which a human heart can pray. The hundreds of millions, or, as General Johnson says, the eighty millions of our people, are crying in misery for want of the things which they need for life, notwithstanding the fact that the country has had, and can have, more than the entire human race can consume.

One hundred and twenty-five million people of America have seated themselves at the barbecue table to eat the products which have been given to them by their Lord and Creator. There is provided by the Almighty what it takes for all of them to eat. Yea, more.

There has been provided for the people of America who have been called to this barbecue table more than is needed for all to eat, but the financial masses of America have taken off of the barbecue table 90 per cent of the food placed thereon by the Lord, even before the feast began. And there is left on that table for 125,000,000 people about what is needed for the 10,000,000. In other words, there is not enough to feed one out of twelve.

What has become of the balance of those victuals placed on the table by the Lord for the use of us all? They are in the hands of the Morgans, the Rockefellers, the Mellons, the Baruchs, the Bakers, the Astors, the Vanderbilts, 600 families at the most, either possessing or controlling the entire 90 per cent of all that is in America.

These big men cannot eat all the food, they cannot wear all the clothes, so they destroy it. They rot it up, they plow it up, they pour it in the river. They bring destruction to the acts of mankind to let humanity suffer, to let humanity go naked, to let humanity go homeless, so that nothing may occur that will do harm to their vanity and to their greed. Like the dog in the manger, they command a wagon load of hay which the dog would not allow the cow to eat, though he could not eat it himself.

So now, ladies and gentlemen, I introduce again, for fear that there are some who have just tuned in and do not know who is talking. This is Huey P. Long, United States Senator from Louisiana, talking over a National Broadcasting Company hookup, from Washington, D.C.

We come to that plan of mine, now, for which I have been so recently and roundly condemned and denounced by the Roosevelt administration and by such men as Mr. Farley and Mr. Robinson and General Hugh S. Johnson, and other spellers and speakers and spoilers.

It is for the redistribution of wealth and for guaranteeing comfort and convenience to all humanity out of this abundance in our country. I hope none will be horror-stricken when they hear me say that we must limit the size of the big men's fortunes in order to guarantee a minimum of fortune, life and comfort to the little man, but if you are horror-stricken at my mention of that fact, think first that such is the declaration on which Mr. Roosevelt rode into nomination and election to President of the United States.

While my urgings are declared by some to be the ravings of a madman and, by such men as General Johnson, as insincere bait for a pied piper, if you will listen to me you will find that it is stating the law handed down by God to man.

You will find that it was the exact provision of the contract of law of the Pilgrim Fathers who landed at Plymouth in 1620. Now, just for the benefit of some of these gentlemen, I am going to read you from the contract of those Pilgrim Fathers who landed at Plymouth in 1620. I am reading you from the contract of those Pilgrim Fathers:

"Paragraph 5: That at the end of the seventh year, the capital and profits, that the houses, lands, goods and chattels be equally divided betwixt the adventurers and planters. When done, every man shall be free from any debt or detriment concerning this adventure."

In other words, these birds who are undertaking to tell you of the bad things I have done and am advocating, they have failed to note that I not only have the Bible back of me, but that this nation was founded by the

Pilgrim Fathers, not to do just what I said, but to go and do all the balance, divide up equally every seventh year and cancel out all debts, and they had the authority of the Bible for doing that. On the other hand, mine does not go near so far, but it will save this country as the Pilgrims intended it should be saved.

You will find that what I am advocating is the cornerstone on which nearly every religion since the beginning of man has been founded. You will find that it was urged by Lord Bacon, by Milton, by Shakespeare in England; by Socrates, by Plato, by Diogenes and the other wisest of the philosophers of ancient Greece; by Pope Pius XI in the Vatican; by the world's greatest inventor, Marconi, in Italy; Daniel Webster, Ralph Waldo Emerson, Abraham Lincoln, Andrew Jackson, William Jennings Bryan and Theodore Roosevelt in the United States, as well as by nearly all of the thousands of great men whose names are mentioned in history, and the only great man who ever came forth to dispute these things from the Bible down is this marvelous General Hugh S. Johnson, who labels himself a soldier and a lawyer.

He is a great soldier though he never smelt powder or heard a cap snap, and a great lawyer though he never tried a lawsuit, and I will not be willing to transact business on the lines that everybody else must be forgotten whom I follow, and if I should follow in such footsteps as was arranged for the combination of an alphabetical proposition.

The principle that I am advocating, that I will give you in detail in a minute, that principle was not only the mainspring of the Roosevelt nomination and election but in the closing speech of Herbert Hoover at Madison Square Garden in November, 1932, even Hoover said:

"My conception of America is a land where men and women may work in liberty, where they may enjoy the advantages of wealth, not concentrated in the hands of the few but diffused through the lives of all."

So there you have it, ladies and gentlemen; both Hoover and Roosevelt swallowed the Huey Long doctrine and never made one single complaint before the election occurred on Nov. 8, 1932.

Now I come to give you again that plan, taken from these leaders of all times and from the Bible, for the sponsoring of which I have been labeled by American men as a madman and pied piper and demagogue, so I give you that plan of our Share Our Wealth Society.

I propose, first, that every big fortune will be cut down immediately. We will cut that down by a capital levy tax to where no one will own more than a few millions of dollars. As a matter of fact, no one can own a fortune in excess of three or four millions of dollars, just between you and me, and I think that is too much. But we figure we can allow that size of a fortune and give prosperity to all the people, even though it is done.

I propose that the surplus of all the big fortunes above a few millions to any one person, at the most, go into the United States ownership. Now, how would we get all these surplus fortunes into the United States Treasury, Mr. Johnson wants to know. Well, now, if he will listen, he won't have any trouble finding out. It is not hard to do. We would not do it by making every one sell what he owned. No. We would send every one a questionnaire, just like they did during the war, when they were taking us over there to make the world safe for democracy so that they might come back here and make America safe for autocracy.

On that questionnaire the man to whom it was sent would list the properties he owned, lands, the houses, stocks and bonds, factories and patents; every man would place an appraisal on his property which the government would review and maybe change. On that appraisal the big fortune holder would say out of what property he would retain the few millions allowed to him, the balance to go to the United States.

Let's say that Mr. Henry Ford should show that he owned all the stock of the Ford Motor Company, and that it is worth $2,000,000,000, we will say. He would claim, say, $4,000,000 dollars of the Ford stock, but $1,996,000,000 would go to the United States.

Say the Rockefeller Foundation was listed at $10,000,000,000 in oil stocks, bank stocks, money and storehouses. Each Rockefeller could say whether he wanted his limit in the money, oil or bank stock, but about $9,900,000,000 would be left and that would go to the United States Government.

And so in this way, this Government of the United States would come into the possession of about two-fifths of the wealth which on normal values would be worth from $165,000,000,000 to $175,000,000,000.

Then we would turn to the inventories of the 25,000,000 families of America and all those showing properties and moneys clear of debt that were above $5,000 and up to the limit of a few millions. We wouldn't draw down a fortune that wasn't bigger than a few millions, and if a man had over $5,000 then he would have his guaranteed minimum. But those showing less than $5,000 for the family, free of debt, would be added to; so that every family would start life again with homestead possession of at least a home and the comforts needed for a home, including such things as a radio and an automobile.

Those things would go to every family as a homestead not to be sold either for debts or for taxes or even by consent of the owner, except the government would allow it, and then only on condition that the court hold it, that is, hold the money that was received for it, to be spent for the purpose of buying another home and the comforts thereof.

Such would mean that the $165,000,000,000 or more taken from the big fortunes would have about $100,000,000,000 of it used to provide everybody with the comforts of home. The government might have to issue warrants for claim and location, or even currency to be retired from such property as it was claimed, but all that is a detail not impractical to get these homes into the hands of the people.

So America would start again with millionaires, but with no multi-millionaires or billionaires; we would start with some poor, but they wouldn't be so poor that they wouldn't have the comforts of life. The lowest a man could go would not take away his home and the home comforts from him.

America, however, would still have a $65,000,000,000 balance after providing these homes. Now what do we do with that? Wait a minute and I will tell you.

Second: We propose that after homes and comforts of homes have been set up for the families of the country, that we will turn our attention to the children and the youth of the land, providing first for their education and training.

We would not have to worry about the problem of child labor, because the very first thing which we would place in front of every child would be not only a comfortable home during his early years, but the opportunity for education and training, not only through the grammar school and the high school, but through college and to include vocational and professional training for every child.

If necessary, that would include the living cost of that child while he attended college, if one should be too distant for him to live at home and conveniently attend, as would be the case with many of those living in the rural areas.

We now have an educational system, and in States like Louisiana, and it is the keystone, where school books are furnished free to every child and where transportation by bus is given to every student, however far he may live from a grammar or high school, there is a fairly good assurance of education through grammar and high school for the child whose father and mother have enough at home to feed and clothe them.

But when it comes to a matter of college education, except in few cases, the right to a college education is determined at this day and time by the financial ability of the father and mother to pay for the cost and the expense of a college education.

It doesn't make any difference how brilliant a boy or girl may be; that doesn't give them the right to a college education in America today.

Now General Hugh Johnson says I am indeed a very smart demagogue, a wise and dangerous menace. But I am one of those who didn't have the opportunity to secure a college education or training.

We propose that the right to education and the extent of education will be determined and gauged not so much by the financial ability of the parents, but by the mental ability and energy of a child to absorb the learning at a college.

This should appeal to General Johnson, who says I am a smart man, since, had I enjoyed the learning and college training which my plan would provide for others, I might not have fallen into the path of the dangerous menace and demagogue that he has now found me to be.

Remember we have $65,000,000,000 to account for that would lie in the hands of the United States, even after providing home comforts for all families. We will use a large part of it immediately to expand particularly the colleges and universities of this country. You would not know the great institutions like Yale, Harvard and Louisiana State University. Get ready for a surprise.

College enrollments would multiply 1,000 per cent. We would immediately call in the architects and engineers, the idle professors and scholars of learning. We would send out a hurry call because the problem of providing college education for all the youth would start a fusilade of employment which might suddenly and immediately make it impossible for us to shorten the hours of labor, even as we contemplate in the balance of our program.

And how happy the youth of this land would be tomorrow morning if they knew instantly their right to a home and the comforts of a home and to complete college and professional training and education were assured. I know how happy they would be, because I know how I would have felt had such a message been delivered to my door.

I cannot deliver that promise to the youth of this land tonight, but I am doing my part. I am standing the blows; I am hearing the charges hurled at me from the four quarters of the country.

It is the same fight which was made against me in Louisiana when I was undertaking to provide the free school books, free buses, university facilities and things of that kind to educate the youth of that State as best I could.

It is the same blare which I heard when I was undertaking to provide for the sick and the afflicted.

When the youth of this land realizes what is meant and what is contemplated, the Billingsgate and the profanity of all of the Farleys and Johnsons in America cannot prevent the light of truth from hurling itself in understandable letters against the dark canopy of the sky.

Now, when we have landed at the place where homes and comforts are provided for all families and complete education and training for all young men and women, the next problem is, what about our income to sustain our people thereafter. How shall that be arranged to guarantee all the fair share of what soul and body need to sustain them conveniently. That brings us to our next point.

We propose:

Third: We will shorten the hours of labor by law so much as may be necessary that none will be worked too long and none unemployed. We will cut hours of toil to thirty hours per week, maybe less; we may cut the working year to eleven months' work and one month vacation, maybe less.

If our great improvement programs show we need more labor than we may have, we will lengthen the hours as convenience requires. At all events, the hours for production will be gauged to meet the market for consumption.

We will need all our machinery for many years because we have much public improvement to do. And further, the more use that we may make of them the less toil will be required for all of us to survive in splendor.

Now, a minimum earning would be established for any person with a family to support. It would be such an earning, on which one, already owning a home, could maintain a family in comfort, of not less than $2,500 per year to every family. . . .

General Johnson says that my proposal is for $5,000 guaranteed earnings to each family, which he says would cost from four to five hundred billions of dollars per year which, he says, is four times more than our whole national income ever has been. Why make such untrue statements, General Johnson? Must you be a false witness to argue your point?

I do not propose $5,000 to each family. I propose a minimum of from $2,000 to $2,500 to each family. For 25,000,000 families that minimum income per family would require from $50,000,000,000 to $60,600,000,000.

In the prosperous days we have had nearly double that for income some years, which allowed plenty for the affluent; but with the unheard prosperity we would have, if all our people could buy what they need, our national income would be double what it has ever been.

The Wall Street writer and statistician says we could have an income of at least $10,000 to every family in goods if all worked short hours and none were idle. According to him, only one-fourth the average income would carry out my plan.

And now I come to the balance of the plan. We propose:

No. 4. That agricultural production will be cared for in the manner specified in the Bible. We would plow under no crops; we would burn no corn; we would spill no milk into the river; we would shoot no hogs; we would slaughter no cattle to be rotted. What we would do is this:

We would raise all the cotton that we could raise, all the corn that we could raise, and everything else that we could raise. Let us say, for example, that we raised more cotton than we could use.

But here again I wish to surprise you when I say that if every one could buy all the towels, all the sheets, all the bedding, all the clothing, all the carpets, all the window curtains, all of everything else they reasonably need, America would consume 20,000,000 bales of cotton per year without having to sell a bale to the foreign countries.

The same would be true of the wheat crop, and of the corn crop, and of the meat crop. Whenever every one could buy the things they desire to eat, there would be no great excess in any of those food supplies.

But for the sake of argument, let us say, however, that there would be a surplus. And I hope there will be, because it will do the country good to have a big surplus. Let us take cotton as an example.

Let us say that the United States will have a market for 10,000,000 bales of cotton, and that we raise 15,000,000 bales of cotton. We will store 5,000,000 bales in warehouses provided by the government. If the next year we raise 15,000,000 bales of cotton and only need 10,000,000, we will store another 5,000,000 bales of cotton, and the government will care for that.

When we reach the year when we have enough cotton to last for twelve or eighteen months we will plant no more cotton for that next year. The people will have their certificates of the government, which they can cash in for that year for the surplus, or if necessary, the government can pay for the whole 15,000,000 bales of cotton as it is produced every year, and when the year comes that we will raise no cotton we will not leave the people idle and with nothing to do.

That is the year when, in the Cotton States, we will do our public improvement work that needs to be done so badly. We will care for the flood-control problems, we will expand the electric lines into rural areas; we will widen roads and build more roads, and if we have a little time left, some of us can go back and attend a school for a few months, and not only learn some things we have forgotten, but we can learn some things that they have found out about that they didn't know anything about when we were children.

Now the example of what we would do about cotton is the same policy we would follow about all other crops. This program would necessitate the building of large storage plants, both heated and cold storage warehouses in all the counties of America, and that building program alone would take up the idle people that America has today.

But the money spent would go for good, and would prevent any trouble happening in the future.

And then there is another good thing. If we would fill these warehouses, then if there were to come a year of famine there would be enough on hand to feed and clothe the people of the nation. It would be the part of good sense to keep a year or two of stock on hand all the time to provide for an emergency, maybe to provide for war or other calamity.

I give you the next step in our program:

No. 5. We will provide for old age pensions for those who reach the age of 60, and pay it to all those who have an income of less than $1,000 per year, or less than $10,000 in property or money.

This would relieve from the ranks of labor those persons who press down the price for the use of their flesh and blood.

Now, the person who reaches the age of 60 would already have the comforts of home as well as something else guaranteed by reason of the redistribution that had been made of things. They would be given enough more to give them a reasonably comfortable existence in their declining days.

However, such would not come from a sales tax or taxes placed upon the common run of people. It would be supported from the taxes levied on those with big incomes and the yearly tax that would be levied on big fortunes so that they would always be kept down to a few million dollars to any one person.

No. 6. We propose that the obligations which this country owes to the veterans of its wars, including the soldiers' bonus, and to care for those who have been either incapacitated or disabled, would be discharged without stint or unreasonable limit.

I have always supported each and every bill that has had to do with the payment of the bonus due to the ex-service men. I have always opposed reducing the allowances which they have been granted. It is an unfair thing for a country to begin its economy while big fortunes exist, by inflicting misery on those who have borne the burden of national defense.

Now, ladies and gentlemen, such is the share our wealth movement. What I have here stated to you will be found to be approved by the law of our Divine Maker. You will find it in the Book of Deuteronomy, from the twenty-fifth to the twenty-seventh chapters. You will find it in the writings of King Solomon. You will find it in the teachings of Christ. You will find it in the words of our great teachers and statesmen of all countries and of all times. If you care to write to me for such proof, I shall be glad to furnish it to you free of expense by mail.

Will you not organize a share our wealth society in your community tonight or tomorrow to place this plan into law? You need it; your people need it. Write me, wire to me; get into this work with us if you believe we are right.

Help to save humanity. Help to save this country. If you wish a copy of this speech or a copy of any other speech I have made, write me and it will be forwarded to you. You can reach me always in Washington, D.C.

REV. CHARLES E. COUGHLIN

Ladies and Gentlemen: I am truly indebted to the National Broadcasting System by whom this time is contributed and to General Hugh Johnson for having provided the occasion and the opportunity for me to address you.

Our concept of government so far transcends the bigotry of race, of creed, of color and of profession to such an extent that through our forefathers we refrained from writing into the Constitution of the United States any impediment to disbar any citizen from engaging in the activities of good citizenship. I am compelled to rehearse this plain truth for your consideration because a demagogic utterance, by appealing to thoughtlessness, to religious and to professional bigotry, has questioned it.

The money changers whom the priest of priests drove from tne temple of Jerusalem both by word and by physical force have marshaled their forces behind the leadership of a chocolate soldier for the purpose of driving the priest out of public affairs.

While always a priest I address you neither as the spokesman of the Catholic Church nor as the representative of its Catholic following. I speak to you as American to American.

The economic disaster which overwhelmed our nation proved beyond question that, independent of all racial or religious differences, there was common need for Catholic, Protestant, Jew and irreligionist to solve a common problem. Together did we not enjoy a common citizenship? Together did we not rejoice in the common appellation of Americans? Together have we not worried through the dark years of this depression? Thus, when through the inevitable sequence of events, a crisis has been reached in the development of our social well-being; when it became necessary to bridge the chasm that separates this day of our economic affliction from the tomorrow of our hoped-for benediction, some one, irrespective of his catholicity or of his protestantism, or of his Jewish faith, was required to raise his voice, if for no other reason than to condemn those who, refusing to leave the land of sorrow, obstructed our passage to the land of prosperity. While it was and always will be impossible for me to divest myself of my Catholic priesthood, nevertheless, in accepting the dignities which my religion conferred upon me I sacrificed in no respect the rights identified with my citizenship. It is still my prerogative to vote. It is still my duty as a common citizen to engage in the common efforts for the preservation of our commonwealth as chaos clamors at our doors. . . .

While always a priest I carry to you the fundamental doctrines of social justice which are intended both for the religionist and irreligionist, for black and white, for laborer and farmer, for everyone who shares with me the citizenship in which I rejoice.

Therefore, away with that prostituted bigotry which at one time has been the poisoned rapier of arrant cowards and at another the butcher's cleaving axe wielded to destroy a national unity.

The object of the National Union for Social Justice is secure economic liberty for our poeple. So well is this truth known that the concentrators of wealth are resorting to musty methods long since in disrepute to preserve America for the plutocrats and to retain its quarreling citizens for their exploitation.

Our program, which is interested in restoring America to the

Americans, can be accomplished peacefully only through a national solidarity. Peacefully, I say, because I believe in the Prince of Peace and dare not disregard His warning that they who use the sword shall perish by it.

In the meantime, therefore, let the Tories of high finance learn from their prototype, George III. Let the unjust aggressors who for generations have mismanaged the economic affairs of our nation assume the entire responsibility of their Tory stubborness. The laborer has not sabotaged our factories! The farmer has not created a man-made scarcity of food! The 80,000,000 cry babies have not concentrated our wealth! These people, played upon by paid-for propaganda did not hurl us into the seething maelstrom of a bloody war.

These cry babies–80,000,000 of them so confessed–were not responsible for the concentration of wealth in the hands of a few and for the destruction of small industry. They did not force 22,000,000 hungry men and women to stand in a bread line nor with the lash of poverty did they drive 11,000,000 laborers into idleness and insecurity.

I am characterized as a revolutionary for raising my voice against these palpable injustices, while the blind Bourbons cannot see the writing on the wall nor read the pages of history written in crimson by pens which were dipped into the bleeding hearts at Concord, Lexington and Valley Forge.

In 1776 Washington and Jefferson and their compatriots had hurled at them the vile epithet of revolutionary. Their lands had been overtaxed. Their laborers and farmers, had been exploited. Their liberties had been denied. Their right to free speech and to petition had been scoffed at. They, too, were called revolutionary.

Today when the rights to life, to liberty and to the pursuit of happiness have been obstructed by an economic system of high finance far more vicious in its implications and results than were the unjust political aggressions of a George III, they who protest against them are classified and indexed with the patriots of 1776.

This, indeed, is a high compliment inadvertently paid by the New Deal's greatest casualty, General Hugh Johnson, who never faced an enemy nor successfully faced an issue.

Today he and the Wall Streeters whom he represents become distorters of history, perverters of logic as they, the unjust aggressors garb themselves in the raiment of patriotism and cast scorn on those who have offered from their misdeeds the scarlet cloak of the rebel. . . .

My Dear General Johnson, I am not important nor are you. But the doctrines which I preach are important. While you were content to vomit your venom upon my person and against my character, the American public is fully cognizant that not once did you dare attack the truths which I teach. I need not condemn you before the court of public opinion. You have condemned yourself. More than that, you have appeared before a jury of 80,000,000 people–your own figures–who through your lack of Christian charity and justice are today prejudiced against you.

Those "cry babies" whose tears have welled to their eyes because you and your kind have lashed them at the pillar of poverty; these brothers and sisters of Christ whom you and your masters have crowned with the thorns of worry and insecurity; these sterling American citizens whom you first fastened to the cross of hunger and nakedness and then pierced their hearts with the spear of exploitation–these inarticulate people for whom I speak will never forget you and your Wall Streeters.

These people, so you have intimated, are rats being led by the Pied Piper. Must that be the metaphor which you employ to describe the wreckage which your kind has created?

My friends, I appeal to your charity, to your good judgment, to your sense of social justice to bear no ill will against General Johnson. Your intelligence informs you that he is but a faithful obedient servant willing to express in his own grotesque manner the thoughts which are harbored in the mind of his master.

Today he appears before us a figure to be pitied and not condemned. He has been cast out of an Administration because he and his plans were failures. Thus, as he appears before you on future occasions remember that he is regarded as a cracked gramaphone record squawking the message of his master's voice.

My dear general, if I am constrained from indicting your person, it is simply because you are the first great casualty of the New Deal experimentation. Whether you know it or not, you are but a political corpse whose ghost has returned to haunt us. Although I believe that your unquiet spirit will not rest in peace, nevertheless, I still believe in that ethical axiom–Of the dead let us speak kindly.

When real soldiers come forth to fight, having facts for targets and truths for ammunition, I shall oppose them with the most forceful weapons which my wits command, but never shall I adopt dishonest tactics or dishonest warfare. I shall draw my reasons from that school of militancy presided over by Jesus Christ, who, 1900 years ago, refrained not from attacking in scathing terms the scribes and pharisees. "Woe to you scribes and pharisees, hypocrites, because you devour the houses of widows, praying long prayers. For this you shall receive the greater judgment. For you bind heavy and insupportable burdens and lay them on men's shoulders; but with a finger of your own you will not move them."

Yes, General Johnson, Christ is accused of stirring class against class by the Voltaires, the Rousseaus, the Louis XVI's, and the atheists of all times. But there are times when certain classes must be forcefully reminded that there is such a thing as Christian charity which bids us love our neighbors as ourselves, and that warns us that whatsoever we do, even to the least, we do to Christ. That is what the Pharisees refused to learn. That is what their descendants in Wall Street refuse to accept as they continue to devour the houses of widows and tax our citizenry into slavery and idleness.

Remembering the method of attack employed by Christ's Precursor, John the Baptist, I will dare confront the Herods by name and by fact even though my head be served on a golden platter, even though my body be sawed in twain as was that of the prophet Isaias for having scorned into disrepute a prince by the name of Manasses.

Today there is another Manasses, your lord and master, General Johnson. I refer to Bernard Manasses Baruch, whose full name has seldom been mentioned, but which name from this day forth shall not be forgotten. This was the name his parents gave him, the name Manasses. This is the name, General Johnson, of your prince of high finance.

Him with the Rothschilds in Europe, the Lazzere in France, the Warburgs, the Kuhn-Loebs, the Morgans and the rest of that wrecking crew of internationalists whose God is gold and whose emblem is the red shield of exploitation–these men I shall oppose until my dying days even though the Bernard Manasses Baruch of Wall Street is successful in doing to me what the prince after whom he was named accomplished in doing to Isaias.

I am well apprised of the fact that your own vociferous volubility, which you characterized last Monday night as "howling," is but the opening gun in a well organized attack against me. I fear it not because I am protected by the moral support of the "cry babies" and the "rats" whom you have forced into the ranks of the National Union for Social Justice. Therefore, I shall doubly bend my efforts to the task of handing back America to the Americans and of rescuing our beloved country from the hands of the internationalists.

There are two remaining charges which you made against me. I rejoice in this opportunity to answer them. The first respects money. You said that my plan is "to make money out of nothing, which would therefore make it worth nothing." At least you admit that I have a plan. I need not inform this audience that since 1930 and long before it I had a plan to establish social justice. Long before you or the financial puppet-masters who are expert in manipulating the strings of Punch and Judy oratory became prominent in the desperate struggle for economic independence I was associated with pioneers who were protesting against the profitless labor of our farmers and against the slavery of modern mass productionism.

Where were you in 1930 and 1931 while we were advocating New Deal on Sundays and feeding thousands in the bread line on Mondays, made necessary by the cold-blooded individualism of an ancient economic system?

Where were you in 1932 when our same group was advocating the election of Franklin D. Roosevelt and the birth of a New Deal long before Franklin Roosevelt was even nominated for the Presidency?

Where were you in 1933 and 1934 when our beloved leader, consecrated to drive the money changers out of the temple, was hampered and impeded by your master, Bernard Manasses Baruch, the acting president of the United States, the uncrowned prince of Wall Street?

I say this in no disparagement because every one appreciates that you are nothing more than his man Friday. With Bernard Manasses Baruch's plan in your pocket to regiment industry, to destroy competition, to institute a wage system designated to share poverty, to create monopolies and eliminate small industries–you strutted upon the stage of this depression like a comic opera general. You organized a comic opera parade on the streets of New York.

Why, General, before your name and underslung vocabulary became household words in this nation, the pioneer associates of mine had been fighting in the front trenches against the enemies of the New Deal, bearing its heaviest burdens, carrying its heaviest crosses.

And now you accuse me of planning to make money out of nothing. But let us become more specific. The man who put this thought into your mouth is nothing but a thief yelling "Stop, thief." Bear with me, General, as I refresh the memory of this audience on the nature of money and how it is manufactured out of nothing by your masters.

1–As you confess, money is merely the medium of trade. It is not wealth; it is only the transportation system, as it were, by which wealth is carried from one person to another.

2–For more than 100 years the people of this nation have permitted a small group of men to possess the privilege of making money and thereby of controlling the flow of wealth. Many of us began to believe that money was the real wealth instead of the trick, as it were, whose only reason for existence is to carry the precious freight of food, of clothing, of shelter of human beings and their labor from one point to another–from the producer to the consumer.

There are many kinds of transportation, such as the railway, the truck, the steamboat. There are three kinds of capitalistic money, all monopolized for use by the banker–metal, paper currency and credit. In round figures, there are $9,000,000,000 of idle metal in the Treasury, $5,500,000,000 of paper currency throughout the nation and at least $250,000,000,000 of credit or of debt money, such as mortgages, loans, bonds, etc. Credit money or pen and ink plus checkbook money is really the major portion of all our money by 90 per cent. Credit money is checkbook money.

3–How is this checkbook money created in this nation? First, a group of wealthy men petition the government for a bank charter, or, in other words, for the right to counterfeit legally.

4–These men deposit, for example, $100,000 with the Treasury. In return, the Treasury gives them $100,000 worth of interest-bearing bonds, which are kept at Washington as security. But the interest accumulating on the bonds belongs to these new bankers.

5–These men return to their home town after they have the government print for them, at scarcely no cost, $100,000 worth of paper dollars, which they deposit in their new bank.

6–John Smith comes to these bankers for a loan of $10,000, which he obtains at 6 per cent on depositing as security the deed for his $20,000 farm.

7–Then the banker gives John a checkbook–no actual cash, mind you–and immediately writes on his own books that $10,000 has been deposited, whereas in truth it was simply loaned.

8–Fifty, eighty, one hundred John Smiths go through the same process until the bank which started with only $100,000 of printed money has loaned $1,000,000 at 6 per cent. That was their rule, to lend ten times what they actually had. Therefore, the first year in business netted the bank $60,000 interest profit on investment of $100,000 which all this time was bearing interest for them through the bonds which they deposited originally at Washington at 4 per cent.

9–Of course, Jim Jones and 1,000 other neighbors of Jim Jones placed their savings in the town bank. They thought that this money was safe and that the bank would surrender it on demand. But Jim did not read the fine print in his bankbook. Had he done so, he would have discovered that he had actually loaned his money to the bankers; that he had become a creditor and, therefore, had to take his chance of getting his money back with all the other creditors and patrons of the bank.

10–Meanwhile, from the bankers' bank, the Federal Reserve Bank, word went out that too much money had been loaned by his fellow-bankers. It was time to call in the loans. It was time to cut down on credit. Thus Henry Doe, the manufacturer, John Smith, the farmer, and Peter Adams, the merchant, all of whom borrowed from the bank, were ordered to pay back in currency money, mind you, what they obtained in checkbook money. Simultaneously, this happened all over the nation. Ten, twenty, thirty billion dollars of loans were called. There were only $5,000,000,000 of currency money in existence. It was an impossible situation. Therefore a depression arose. The deeds and mortgages were claimed by the bankers and homes and farms and industries were confiscated by him because there was no currency money.

11–Did the banker close up shop? He did not. At least the big banker did not. They liquidated the homes and farms and industries which they confiscated when the borrowers had no currency money to save them. They sold them for what they could obtain on depressed market. Then they turned around with this new fresh currency money and bought government bonds at 4 per cent or less.

12–Meanwhile, bread lines were established. Unemployment was rife. Poverty stalked through the nation. Of necessity the government must obtain money to feed the poor and must undertake public work to salvage the unemployed. Therefore, it borrowed $8,000,000,000 from the bankers who, playing their game even in the face of an national distress, loaned the government a fat check book and perhaps, for good measure, a bottle of ink and a fountain pen. Still there were only $5,000,000,000 of actual currency in the nation. But, through a banker's magic and a gambler's instinct, they loaned the $8,000,000,000 because they knew that in eighteen years hence, $6,000,000,000 in interest would be returned by the government for the privilege of using a banker's check book—$14,000,000,000 in all.

There, General, is the true story of how money is made out of nothing. Can you or any Wall Streeter controvert this?

To this process of manufacturing money I have been opposed simply because our Constitution says that it is the right of Congress to coin and regulate the value of money. In the year 1694 this right still belonged to the British people and to their Parliament but, when threatened by invasion, the merchants and goldsmiths of London forced Parliament to surrender this right to them. This was the price of their patriotism. This was the birthday of the privately-owned bank of England.

During the days of our Civil War, when Abraham Lincoln was engaged in realizing a dream that was born in the crib at Bethlehem, he needed gold to purchase arms and ammunition. In that day, the international bankers were willing to loan gold to Lincoln on the one condition that he would abrogate and cancel Article 1, Section VIII, Clause V of our Constitution, which says Congress has the right to coin and regulate the value of money. This right they themselves coveted; this right they themselves demanded.

From that day forward until 1913, when the Federal Reserve Banking system was created—a system owned by a group of your masters and not by the American people, as many in this audience formerly believed—from that day forward the economic destinies of our country have been controlled by these private central bankers who extended and contracted credit at will.

Because I have, in season and out of season, demanded that we Americans go back to the Constitution and restore to Congress its right and duty to coin and regulate the value of money you have assailed me and in doing so have stultified yourself.

When did I ever propose to make money out of nothing? I have pointed to $9,000,000,000 of idle gold and silver sterilized in the vaults of our Treasury. I have questioned time after time the wisdom on the part of our government running to the Federal Reserve Bank for dollars created out of nothing, borrowing this manufactured money for relief purposes, for public works activities, with the understanding that the bankers would be repaid either with good currency, at interest, or else the security of the United States could be confiscated by them.

I have advocated that the government employ this idle gold and silver instead of building up unpayable debts to be shouldered by the unborn children of future generations. You and your group have been the inflationists, the makers of money out of nothing. But mindful of the Federal Reserve act, which was passed in 1913, and which permits 2½ currency dollars to be printed against each gold dollar, mindful that we have only $5,250,000,000 paper dollars in the country and over $9,000,000,000 of gold and silver in the Treasury, I have asked and I still ask why we do not employ it for the welfare of the American people instead of utilizing the bankers' manufactured money for the welfare of the Warburgs, the Rothschilds, the Kuhn-Loebs, the Morgans, and your own master, Bernard Manasses Baruch? . . .

The real enemies who are boring from within have been you and your group of Wall Streeters, of international bankers. Who have been the President's advisers over a period of two years? Not the farmer or the laborer, not the National Union for Social Justice, not his close and disinterested friends. Surely they were not responsible for 11,000,000 men who are still unemployed, for 22,000,000 persons who are still in the breadlines, for our national debt which has risen to the unscalable heights of $34,000,000,000. If our people are growing disheartened it is not because they have lost faith in Franklin D. Roosevelt, but because they are rising in their wrath against you and your group who have surrounded him.

It was Bernard Manasses Baruch and the international bankers who whispered into his perturbed ears the philosophy of destruction, the sophistry of social reforms and policies, all of which have prevented a magnificent leader from rescuing a nation still bound to the rock of depression by the chains of economic slavery. Did they not, in season and out of season, obstruct him from driving the money changers from the temple?

My friends in this audience, I still proclaim to you that it is either Roosevelt or ruin. I support him today and will support him tomorrow, because we are neither going back to the individualism of the past nor are we going forward to the communism of the future. But I am not that type of false friend who, mangling the very meaning of the word, praise policies when criticism is required or betray my millions of supporters throughout the nation by preaching to them the prostituted slogan of "peace, peace," when there is no peace. . . .

9
WHAT IS COMMUNISM? A GLIMPSE OF SOVIET AMERICA
Earl Browder*

In the summer of 1935 the American Communist Party adopted the strategy of the popular front. Following the line laid out by Georgi Dimitrov, a Bulgarian communist, party leaders decided that it was necessary to work together with liberal groups in order to defeat the main enemy: fascism. Consequently, communists abandoned their tough, revolutionary posture and devoted their energies instead to achieving piecemeal reform, forging alliances with socialists and third parties, and working in labor unions. Where they had once damned the New Deal as a scheme to fasten shackles on the working class, they now gave strong backing to much of Roosevelt's domestic program. The man who led the party during these years was Earl Browder, who had been born in Wichita, Kansas, in 1891. Browder left school at the age of nine, and served a prison sentence during World War I for refusing to register for the draft. He then helped organize the Communist Party, moving steadily up through the ranks until he became General Secretary, a post he held until shortly after World War II. "Since when is revolution un-American?" Browder asked. "Our country was born and preserved in revolutionary struggles. . . . We Communists are proud that we can truly say that Communism is the Americanism of the twentieth century." In an article published just before the popular front strategy was accepted, Browder outlined the communist blueprint for the future. How does he answer the charge that communism would create a new ruling class and an oppressive conformity? What assumptions about human nature and social organization underlie Browder's position? □

Scores of questions have been put to us asking, in one form or another, what a Soviet America would look like. There is a great temptation to answer with an imaginative picture of the glories of an America released from capitalist sabotage. But the imagination is staggered by the first

---

*Browder, Earl, What Is Communism? A Glimpse of Soviet America, *New Masses,* XVI (July 9, 1935), 9-10.

approach to this task. And, after all, of more value is the sober examination of those objective facts of the already achieved productive forces, to see what can be done even without going a step farther than the technical achievements of capitalism.

To what extent can we take the experience of the Soviet Union as a forecast of what a Soviet America would look like?

In certain respects it gives us an accurate forecast; in other respects the question in America will be placed quite differently. The principles upon which a Soviet America would be organized would be the same, in every respect, as those which have guided the Soviet Union. But in our case, these principles would be applied, not to the most backward but to the most advanced capitalist country. This makes for tremendous differences in the physiognomy of the new society.

In Russia the actual seizure of power and establishment of the Soviet Government was relatively easy and almost bloodless; only afterward came the imperialist intervention, prolonged civil war and capitalist-inspired wrecking which, added to the ruin the World War inflicted upon a backward country, left the Soviet Government with the task of building from the ground up in the midst of a hostile world.

In America most of our difficulties lie precisely in the achievement of power for the working class, in the establishment of the Soviet Government; after that has been accomplished, the American capitalists will have no great powerful allies from abroad to help them continue the struggle; it will *already* be clear that world capitalism has received its death-blow; and the Soviet Government of America will take over a society already technically prepared for Communism. Where in Russia it was necessary to go through the prolonged period of War Communism, the N.E.P., the First and Second Five Year Plans, in America we will *start* economically at a stage further advanced, at about the point which Russia will reach in her Fourth Five Year Plan.

The only thing that could change this basic perspective for America would be a possible, but unpredictable, destruction of American economy by an imperialist war, carried out by agencies of destruction hitherto unknown.

The United States, in short, contains already all the prerequisites for a Communist society except the single factor of Soviet Power. In Russia, Lenin said, several years after 1917, "The Soviet Power, plus electrification, equals Communism." In America the electrification already exists, so we can shorten Lenin's formulas.

The question is, then, given the American working class in undisputed power, what would be the possible and probable course of development of the economic and social life of the country?

The new government would immediately take over and operate all the banks, railroads, water and air transports, mines and all major trustified industries. Minor industries, municipal public utilities and the distributive occupations would be reorganized as functions of local government or as cooperatives or, in some instances, as auxiliaries of major industries. Large-scale agriculture would be taken over and operated by the government, while the mass of small farms would be encouraged to combine into voluntary cooperatives for large-scale production with state aid.

All available man-power would be put to work immediately, first of all in the direct production of material wealth, second in its distribution and third in the social services of health, education and entertainment.

Every able-bodied person would be required to go to work and for this receive wages according to a scale socially determined. Such a wage-scale might range, for example, from a minimum of $2,000 per year up to $10,000 or higher, at present values. The average, according to the most conservative estimates of present capacity, after making allowance for capital accumulation, would be about $5,000 per year for each family in the United States. That can be taken as the immediate minimum standard of living under a Soviet Government in America.

In what form would this be made available to the population? Many questions have been raised, asking whether there would not be such regimentation, such monotonous uniformity, even with such high standards measured in volume, as to take the salt out of life. Such doubters visualize the citizens of Soviet America living in uniform barracks, wearing uniform clothing prescribed by law, eating the same meals, reading the same books and newspapers, seeing the same entertainments, thinking the same thoughts, etc., etc. That picture of Communist society is the bogey-man created by the propagandists for capitalism, but the closest that humanity will ever get to such a stage is the present moment under capitalism. These gentlemen would have us believe that Communism will merely take the worst features of capitalism and make it the universal rule. Why we should do such stupid things, no one can explain.

The fact is, of course, that Communist reality would be quite different from this doleful picture. For the first time we could escape from the terrible housing imposed by capitalism and begin to get modern, decent homes for everybody. Even the first simple redistribution of existing housing would revolutionize this situation. We could smash the uniformity of clothing imposed by the combination of our own poverty and capitalist mass production. For the first time in our lives the majority could eat what their tastes dictate, because for the first time they could afford it. And for the first time, the human mind would be liberated from the slavery to Hollywood, Hearst and Co.

Why can we be sure that we would have all these desirable things? Because there would be nothing to prevent us from having them if we want them. We would have the power to form our lives the way we choose; we have every reason, therefore, to expect that the choice will not be stupid, reactionary nonsense described by the enemies of Communism.

The primary concern of the Soviet Government will be *production*; this will be highly centralized, to realize the benefits of the highest technical achievements. All means of production will be socialized, taken out of private control. But the *consumption* will be socialized only upon a voluntary basis, with the greatest flexibility and freedom of choice for each individual. And the greater grows the flow of *production* of wealth, the more complete will become the *freedom of consumption,* up to the point where all consumption will become absolutely free and unfettered.

Only under such a society can we expect to witness the full unfolding of the marvelous potentialities of the human spirit, the development of human genius and individuality raised to the *n*th power because it is the power no longer of a few exceptional individuals but of the million masses of free men and women.

Many of our questioners have asked: "But how can the industries be kept operating at capacity without the profit motive? Will not a bureaucratic apparatus grow up in control which will become a new ruling class? And do we not have again the seeds of the old profit motive in the unequal wages, etc., which even you admit will exist under socialism?" We expect our socialist factories to produce at top speed, precisely because the "profit motive" has been eliminated. That famous old profit motive, which used to open up factories in the youth of capitalism, operates in modern times mainly to close them down. The administrative apparatus of a socialist economy can never become a new ruling class, because it lacks precisely that *private ownership,* that monopoly of the means of life of the masses, which is the foundation of class divisions in society.

No, the old profit motive is not creeping back into the socialist society through the unequal wages, etc. The profit motive has nothing to do with wages, equal or unequal, not withstanding Mr. Roosevelt's efforts in his message to Congress last January, to picture the whole population of the country as living on profits and depending upon increased profits for an increased standard of living. Such a conception of profits belongs not to the literature of economics, but that of the bedtime stories for children. Profit is only that appropriation from the current production of society which is based upon and justified by, the *private ownership* of the socially-used means of production. The profit-motive is never anything else than that motive of the *owners,* as owners, to allow their property to be used for production in the expectation of realizing an increasing proportion of the product as profit. The motive of those who do the producing never was, is not and can never be, a "profit-motive" but exists only in spite of profit and in constant antagonism to it. The removal of profit under socialism releases the basic human motives to labor from their greatest handicap.

What are the human motives to labor? The most primitive and almost the only ones under capitalism are the fear of hunger and want, the desire to escape starvation. Under capitalism, the highest development of this motive is the ambition to rise, by hard labor, out of the laboring class into the petty-bourgeoisie. Under socialism, this most primitive motive will be applied mainly in the remaking of bourgeois elements into workers. For the main mass of workers, socialism introduces new motives, social motives, the motives of social emulation, the honor and heroism of producers serving society and not private profit-takers.

Under socialism, labor becomes more and more of a privilege instead of a burden; it carries with it its own rewards, of which the material aspect becomes less and less important, the aspect of social recognition becomes more and more dominant.

And what a gigantic motive-power for society is this new motive of socialist labor! What an expansion of the human powers is brought about by it! Already the Soviet Union has given us a few glimpses into the profound revolution in human nature that is brought about by the operation of this new motive in human activity.

Socialism is not only a revolution in economic life. It makes an entirely new human race. It takes this man who has been brutalized and degraded through the ages by the violence and oppression of class societies, frees him from this woeful heritage, carries over from the past only the achievements of the human mind and not its crimes and stupidities and remakes man, molding him in the heat of socialist labor into the new social being.

The rising socialist system in the Soviet Union has, for years now, demonstrated that in the expansion of material production it outdistances capitalism in the period of its youth by seven or eight-fold. In the production of superior types of human beings, the superiority of socialism is demonstrated a thousand times more decisively. Capitalism, even in decay, can still produce material wealth, even though the amount becomes smaller; but in the production of higher types of men and the raising of the social level of the production as a whole, the capitalist system has completely lost what power it had in its youth; today it is corrupting and degrading whole populations and poisons and stultifies its own geniuses.

Today it has become clear that all human progress is possible only in struggle against the capitalist system and its agents, only in the fight for socialism as the next stage in the historical march toward the classless, communist society.

10
THE TOWNSEND PLAN
Norman Thomas*

No group of Americans was harder hit by the depression than the elderly. By 1935 perhaps half of the 7.5 million people over 65 were dependent on public support or the charity of their relatives. Many who thought they had put aside enough for retirement found their savings wiped out and their pensions inadequate. They also found it increasingly difficult to fall back on their children who were themselves in many cases out of work. The most popular proposal to aid the elderly came, appropriately, from California—the state where the problem was most severe. It was devised by Dr. Francis E. Townsend, who recommended that all persons over 60 receive $200 a month on the condition that they spend it and agree to retire if employed. This plan would pump money into the economy, open up jobs for younger people, and restore a measure of dignity to old age. Townsend never spoke of a dole; rather, the elderly would act as trustees, spending their money for the general welfare. In the mid-1930's Townsend clubs sprang up across the nation and their popularity aided passage of the Social Security Act. But most of Townsend's followers, believing that the Act did not go nearly far enough, favored independent political action. In 1936 they joined forces with Father Coughlin and with those who had inherited Huey Long's machine after the Louisiana politician's assassination, and nominated William Lemke for president on the Union Party ticket. While the Townsend plan appealed to the elderly because it held out hope for immediate salvation without tampering with the capitalist system, it was precisely for this reason that the veteran socialist leader Norman Thomas considered the plan a mirage. In the Fall of 1936, addressing a Townsend club convention, Thomas provided an orthodox socialist appraisal of one of the panaceas that Americans found so appealing. The point in his speech at which applause gave way to catcalls was the point at which socialism diverged from political messianism. ☐

---

*Thomas, Norman, The Townsend Plan and Cough Drops, *Vital Speeches,* II (September 1, 1936), 755-58. Reprinted by permission of *Vital Speeches of the Day.*

Let me begin by expressing my deep appreciation of the sense of Americanism and fair play which has moved this convention to invite the Presidential candidates of various parties to appear before you.

I am well aware that you are a non-partisan body in so far as you are a convention. That is, I understand that you have not endorsed and do not intend to endorse any party candidate for president or vice-president of the United States. That, may I say, is as it should be. [*Applause and cheering.*]

I do not come before you, therefore, to ask for an endorsement, as a convention, for the Socialist Party. I come before you to talk to you as individual Americans about the claims of the Socialist Party, and about its relation to the Townsend Plan itself.

If I were to take a text–and I understand that texts are popular here–[*laughter*] it would be, "Come now, let us reason together."

If I have read the papers correctly you have had plenty of steam these hot days. The engine is boiling, the boilers are full and the pressure runs high. I cannot hope to add to that steam or to that pressure, but I would like to know where the engine is going to go, and that is a thing I should like to talk to you about for the few minutes that I shall take.

Let me say at the beginning that there are many things with which I find myself in agreement. As I sat here looking over this great audience, I noticed a banner in the back, which says:

> "The Townsend Goal:
> Training for Youth
> Work for Maturity
> Security for Old Age."

That is a magnificent goal which I can most heartily endorse myself. [*Applause and cheering.*] The Socialist Party has been working a long time toward that great goal.

I can endorse also the expression that has often come from you in favor of democracy, but here I have a question to raise. If I am correctly informed, one of your great leaders is the Reverend Gerald L. K. Smith, of Louisiana, and I hope Mr. Smith perhaps can satisfy me on something before I leave. I want to know how Mr. Smith expects his candidate, Mr. Lemke, to be on the ballot in the State of Louisiana. The State of Louisiana, long controlled by Mr. Smith's hero, Huey Long, is perhaps the state where it is hardest of all states for a minority party to get on the ballot. It has been so for years, and years, and years. Even Robert

LaFollette could not get on the ballot in 1924. How is Mr. Lemke going to get on?

And I would like to ask this convention, whatever you think about candidates, isn't it fair in America that minority parties should be on the ballot without such difficulties as to make it impossible? Whatever differences I might have with Mr. Lemke, who is to address you tomorrow, I venture to say that he and I would agree that while there ought to be reasonable rules for getting on the ballot such laws as require 327,000 signatures in Ohio, such laws as prevail in Louisiana, such laws as prevail in North Carolina and in Florida make it impossible to get on the ballot fairly, or at best you can only get on as an independent, or perhaps have your name written in. Even that cannot be done in Louisiana.

May I ask you, not as partisans, but as Americans, if you mean what you say about democracy, mean what you say about dictatorship, why in God's name don't you give us democracy in the states where you live? [*Applause and cheering.*]

And that is the first appeal I make to you.

There is a second appeal I want to make to you: I would like you to consider the situation with regard to judicial supremacy in America. I know some of your leaders who have given much thought on the matter won't agree with me, but I should like solemnly to warn you, with the present Constitution as interpreted by the present Supreme Court of the United States, I do not know any formula for adequate legislation for the goal set forth in that banner opposite me which has a chance to be enacted and to remain constitutional.

I know what the Republicans say: "If after vague further trial, we can't do anything, then maybe we will favor an amendment, giving the states the right to do something." The states aren't big enough to grapple with poverty in America. And the Democratic Platform says that if after further trial it becomes necessary, there will be—what? A "clarifying amendment." Why, the Court has been kicking that New Deal around for two years, it has declared eight out of ten laws unconstitutional. And the Democrats say now, if you keep this up, we will have to clarify it somehow as to where you can kick us.

It seems to me that if you people want what you say you want, whether you agree with Socialists on everything, I have a right to appeal to you to help us to enact in orderly fashion, the Farmers' and Workers' Right Amendment, which gives specifically to the Congress of the United States the power to enact the economic and social legislation which the American people believe to be necessary for their well being. [*Applause.*]

There is no defense of a democracy which leaves the final decision in matters of this sort, to a court, to a majority of the nine men who sit on the Supreme Court.

I think I can ask your support in these matters without appearing partisan.

And there is another great matter in which I am sure that you and I agree. You and I both know that we live in a country where poverty is unnecessary and inexcusable. We both know that we live in a country where we have the means to produce abundance. Here I can quote a conservative authority. The Brookings Institution, in its famous report on America's Capacity to Produce, said that in the year 1929, a really efficient use of our then capacity to produce would have resulted in the production of enough goods so that every family income in the United States could be raised to the two thousand mark without even cutting off any at the top—which also would have been worth doing. There were in the year 1929—that year of our greatest so-called prosperity—16,400,000 American families with less than two thousand a year.

Even as I stand here in this great hall I can see them, the share croppers of the cotton country, living in shacks unfit for hogs, the dwellers in the ugly steel regions through which I came this morning, the men and women in the slums of the great cities, the tenant farmers and the agricultural workers, even in a high and prosperous state like California. Less than two thousand a year? Why, less than one thousand dollars, less than five hundred a year, in this land where we have been paying farmers not to produce crops, the children of the cotton growers go in rags, undernourished with the food that breeds pellagra—a disease of malnutrition.

Dr. Mordecai Ezekiel, a great statistician, has written a book called "Twenty-five Hundred Dollars a Year." He has a plan which I do not think is practical, to manage capitalism so as to get $2,500 a year for each worker. But what is convincing is the first chapter or two in Dr. Ezekiel's book where he gives the figures to support the statement that, properly managed, our resources and our technological equipment would be enough to produce $2,500 a year for each worker.

I am not a poet, and I have not time to try for any special eloquence, but there is something the matter with your understanding, yes, and your imagination, if the thought of what that abundance might mean in America does not thrill you more than any words of poetry or any music can do. We can have that abundance! [*Applause.*]

But please remember, we are thinking things over. I haven't much time, I want you to go on with your program, let me get through, save the applause—save the boos if you want to—to the end.

Now let's think a little bit. Let's talk a little bit about what the Socialist Party thinks is necessary to get this abundance. We say there is no short cut to it under the Capitalist system. We say that you cannot let private individuals own the oil, the coal, the iron, the copper, the dairy trust, the banking system, the great industries of America, and by any device whatsoever, get the abundance that you ought to expect. We say that profits—which the profit system rests upon—depends upon the exploitation of the labor of men and women, labor with hand and brain, in profession, in factory, in town, in country, in mine, in shop. We say moreover that profit always depends on relative scarcity.

I believe that the President of the United States honestly meant what he said when he talked about the abundant life, but the only thing the President of the United States could think of under capitalism was to pay men not to produce to subsidize scarcity, and call it prosperity. And do you say that is the President's fault? I tell you no! That is the fault of the capitalist system, a system which rests upon relative scarcity for its profits. [*Applause.*] Well, I am glad to see I have that many friends; I hope you will remember what I say now! Listen.

Therefore we say that the war for abundance, the struggle for freedom and the struggle for peace depends upon ending the system which rests upon exploitation, upon relative scarcity, the system we know as capitalism.

Now that is a job, but it is not an impossible job. While we are doing that job of establishing in orderly fashion a new and brotherly system, there is a lot we can do for men and women now. We are promising you no distant feast in Utopia on condition that you will starve now. We are promising you that if you will organize your unions, your co-operatives, your political party, you can win abundance. We are promising you that you can master machinery and carry out the dreams of the patriarchs, the sages, the prophets of all ages in the production and sharing of abundance. But it is a job to be done, and we don't think that job can be done—I am telling you now frankly, understand—by the proposal that is so dear to your hearts.

We believe that capitalism can pay a much bigger old age pension than the President's "insecurity" Bill proposes. [*Applause.*] We Socialists have always said that. We are pioneers for old age pensions. I have heard Democrats admit it when they finally gave us a bad law in New York.

They said—"Well, of course the Socialists always advocated this, but it took us to finish it."—Yes, they finished it—they finished it the wrong way. We are for a bigger pension than is now paid in any state. In principle we are for the Frazier-Lundeen Bill for security for the aged, the unemployed, and the invalid.

Why do I then say "No" to the Townsend Plan? I will tell you. Because I don't think you can keep capitalism and make the capitalist system pay you twice as much for not working when you are sixty as you got on the average for working before you were sixty. I think you have got to begin by saying: pay workers what they earn and make that cardinal in your program. [*Applause.*]

Wait a minute, I have only a little time and I have got to go fast:

You say—keep capitalism—some of you say—and just give us this pension. Do you think you can perform vivisection on Wall Street? Do you think that capitalism, not killed, will stand still while by legislative fiat you pay to some seven or eight per cent of the population an amount which in 1935 would have been equal to between a third and a half of the national income?

You can conquer capitalism, you can take power in the state for a new system, but you cannot keep capitalism and do this trick—I don't think so and I am being honest with you. Moreover, I don't think you can raise $200 a month by a two per cent cash transaction tax. [*The convention booed the speaker.*]

All right, I am glad to know what you think and I expected that. [*Laughter.*] Now you have told me, and I will tell you why you say that, and I will tell you why I say what I say.

I wish you could cure everything by a revolving pension. I would be a happy man if I thought that all you had to do was that. Life would be much easier for me. It is because I don't think it that I will tell you so.

My friends, Dr. Townsend is a physician. There must have been many times when a man came to him with tuberculosis and wouldn't admit it, and some friend said, "Just try this cough drop and you will be all right." Dr. Townsend, I suppose said, "My friend, I am sorry for you, you can get well, but you cannot do it by this cough drop."

Right or wrong, I feel about this plan of yours the way he felt in a case like that. I tell you that you can get well, but cannot get well under the capitalist system, by this particular method.

Why?

Who is going to pay that two per cent tax? [*The convention booed.*]

Wait a minute. How many people are there– . . . [*The convention would not be in order.*]

By the way, Father Coughlin spoke to you and you cheered him to the echo, but Father Coughlin never to my knowledge retracted the statement that he made that branded this plan as "economic insanity." Why not ask him what he thinks of the plan? And don't forget to ask Mr. Lemke.

I am going on–I am saying that this tax is a transaction tax, and that there are many transactions between the farmer that breeds the sheep and the coats you and I wear, and if you and I have to pay the two per cent on each, you and I will have more taxes to pay than coats on our backs. [*The convention continued to boo the speaker.*]

Dr. Townsend: Friends, please let us show courtesy to a man whom we have invited. Please be quiet. [*Applause and cheering.*]

Mr. Thomas: I want to thank you, Dr. Townsend, for that, but I have no reproaches to make to any of you, I am talking frankly and you are talking back. Let me go on and we will soon be through.

I am saying that the reason I take the stand I do is that as candidate for President of the United States I cannot endorse the possibility of the effectiveness of the Townsend Plan, that is $200 a month financed by a cash transaction tax, first because I don't think the money can be raised, second because when it cannot be raised by a tax that will ruin consumers, you are likely to get inflation which will make $200 equal to about $20 in purchasing power as it once happened in France. [*The convention booed.*]

Third, because I think you are taking your magnificent enthusiasm and your time, and using it when you might use it more profitably for your real emancipation.

One more word and I am done.

I was concerned the other day at the nature of the attack that Father Coughlin made on the President. I am fighting the Democratic Party, I am fighting the Republican Party, but I do not think America is going to be helped by a campaign of personal hate and bitterness. [*Applause and cheering.*]

As nearly as I make out, President Roosevelt followed Father Coughlin's advice in devaluing the dollar; it wasn't bad advice. Why does Father Coughlin blame him so severely when it hasn't worked miracles? Why doesn't Father Coughlin outline precisely the kind of plan which would finance relief and not create debt? I can do it as a Socialist, I can tell you about the capital levy, but if I believed in capitalism I would have my own troubles doing that.

Why, by the way hasn't Father Coughlin talked more constructively? I ask you, whatever you think of the Socialist Party or of me, to think of these things for the sake of America and for the sake of the future, for which all of us care.

And one last thing: All over the United States people have said to me that one reason for the objection to President Roosevelt on the part of Father Coughlin is Father Coughlin's feeling that President Roosevelt did not intervene sufficiently in Mexico on behalf of the Roman Catholic Church. [*Applause mixed with boos.*]

I believe in religious freedom; I believe in protest against every breach of religious freedom, but I do not believe in intervention in Mexico under any pretext whatsoever. I want now to ask Mr. Lemke, tomorrow, or Mr. Landon, to say whether or not they will support the President's policy of non-intervention in Mexico. And that is a question I have a right to ask.

And now I come to the end. You don't agree with me, most of you. I wish you did. Any candidate would be glad to have an audience like this agree with him. You don't suppose I stand up here and talk with you frankly because it is fun. Do you think I don't know how to make speeches you would applaud? I would not have to tell you that I didn't agree with you in every respect. I could make a speech about liberty, about freedom, about abundance, about "down with the bankers"–I can make them, and they would be true.

But I want to talk honestly with you, my American friends, and I want to say to you there is freedom and peace and plenty, there is a conquest of poverty, there is leisure, there is emancipation from the power of monopolistic control. It is an emancipation, a freedom, a peace, a plenty you have got to win by nothing less than by making America yours, by taking collectively and co-operatively the great sources of wealth into your hands and managing them democratically for the common good.

Let the experts work for you and not for the private owners. Let that be your slogan, and I think then that we shall win such victories as the imagination of man has scarcely dared to dream; I think then we shall break down the dark prison house of poverty; I think then we shall break the shackles which now bind our freedom in a world where the few own what the many need.

I congratulate you on your purpose. I congratulate you on the democracy which has let me speak to you. I plead with you, stand for that democracy all the way against every sign of dictatorship. If you must support Lemke, make the Lemke party democratic and not merely something born over the radio. Stand for that democracy and though we disagree today, the time may come that we shall meet on some glorious field of victory for plenty, for peace, for freedom, for the emancipation of youth from toil, and old age from fear.

I thank you. [*The convention cheered and applauded.*]

11
THE CREED OF MODERN CHRISTIAN SOCIALISTS
Reinhold Niebuhr*

Perhaps no one has exerted a more important influence upon modern liberal and radical thought than Reinhold Niebuhr. Upon graduation from the Yale Divinity School in 1915 Niebuhr served as a pastor in Detroit and then, in 1928, took a position at the Union Theological Seminary in New York. In *Moral Man and Immoral Society* (1932), he attempted to distinguish between the behavior of individuals and that of social groups: while individuals could act in a moral way ("in the sense that they are able to consider interests other than their own in determining problems of conduct"), society could not. Since "more unrestrained egoism" characterized societal behavior, those who sought to perfect society would have to adopt less-than-perfect means. In 1932 Niebuhr still believed that of all social groups the proletariat was best able to transcend narrow self interest; but as the decade wore on he gradually became more skeptical. Even while he voted the socialist ticket during the 1930's Niebuhr expressed doubts about the Marxist position. Rejecting the Marxian claim that "man's sinfulness is the consequence of a faulty social organization," he could not "hope for the redemption of man by the mere reorganization of society." Socialization of private property, while desirable in itself, would not destroy the "sinful will-to-power" in men or nations. Writing in his journal, *Radical Religion,* in 1938, Niebuhr explained why religion could serve radical as well as conservative purposes, why orthodox Marxism appeared "utopian," and why no form of social organization could "achieve perfect equality." How do Niebuhr's views regarding human nature and social organization compare with those of Earl Browder? In what sense, if any, can it be said that Niebuhr remained a "socialist"? □

While Marxians regard religion as constitutionally conservative and "counterrevolutionary," reactionaries like the late Oswald Spengler think

---

*Niebuhr, Reinhold, The Creed of Modern Christian Socialists, *Radical Religion* (Spring, 1938), 13-18. Reprinted by permission of Reinhold Niebuhr.

of radicalism as a kind of illegitimate offspring of Christianity. It was Spengler's theory that revolutionary radicalism was the consequence of the moral confusion of certain priests of religion, who took the absolute demands of the gospels too seriously or, at least, too politically. Instead of inculcating a proper otherworldliness in the heart of the faithful, which would help them to bear their mortal pains with patience, these priests falsely interpreted the ideals of religion as possible achievements of the political order.

This criticism of religion from two absolutely contradictory perspectives is a little confusing to the casual observer. It accords nevertheless with the actual relation of religion to the social problem. Religion is at once the most conservative and the most radical force in social life. It is the most conservative when it gives any given social order the aura of religious sanctity and insists that rebels against a "Christian" civilization are rebels against God. It is the most radical force when its conceptions of an unconditioned good become the principle of criticism for the dubious social realities of a particular social and economic system. Stated in traditional concepts it is conservative when it falsely identifies its "kingdom of God" with the relative achievements in justice of the kingdoms of this world. It is radical when loyalty to the "kingdom of God," the vision of a pure and unconditioned justice and love creates dissatisfaction with the imperfect love and justice of any given economic and political order.

Naturally the conservative tendencies in any organized expression of religion are more dominant than the radical ones. Every organized spiritual life becomes intimately related, by the necessities of its physical organism, to the social order in which it lives. Consciously and unconsciously it conforms to the peculiar prejudices of the dominant social groups. This is just as true of organized education as of organized religion. It is one of the peculiar vagaries of Marxism to regard religion as inherently conservative while the total educational process of society is regarded as conservative only as long as it remains under the dominance of the capitalistic classes.

The fact is that religion has resources of rebellion against any status quo which a secular culture does not possess. Secular culture can always be betrayed by its relativism into conformity with a given system of power. When Pilate sneers, "What is truth?" the liberal relativist does not always know the answer and ends by conforming to the truth which Caesar and Pilate have made true by their power. Thus the German university, seat and symbol of German liberalism, has been "coordinated" to Naziism, though, of course, many brave spirits in it refused to conform and are now in exile. The German church, on the other hand refused to conform as an institution; or, at least, there is a significant minority in the church which refuses to conform. Unlike the academic minority it expresses itself in organizational rather than purely individual terms. Its watchword is "We must obey God rather than man." That watchword is the perfect symbol and proof of the social resource of an ultimate and transcendent reference for our loyalties. Those who believe in the sovereignty of God can never give unqualified allegiance to temporal sovereignties. This is a perpetual source of rebellion and radicalism in religion, though it must be admitted that a large proportion of the faithful always find ways of transferring the sanctity of the divine to temporal rulers, who become "vice-regents" of Christ and kings by "divine right."

Because of this resource the Christian church has always possessed some kind of "left wing." During the period of the Reformation the Anabaptists and sectaries constituted this left wing. In the Cromwellian period the Fifth Monarchy men, levellers and diggers, composed the revolutionary left wing of his army. Modern Marxian radicalism is in fact a secularized version of this proletarian and peasant discontent as it expressed itself in apocalyptic sects throughout history. The hope of these sects was always the "kingdom of God on earth" rather than purely individualistic hopes of fulfillment in terms of personal immortality.

Since the middle of the nineteenth century Christian radicalism has been the expression of an uneasy conscience in the middle classes, rather than a vent for proletarian discontent, Protestantism having become an essentially middle class religion. As a consequence it accepted the general presuppositions of liberalism, which is the real religion of middle class life. It believed in progress and abhorred the possibility of catastrophe in history. It identified the kingdom of God with the idea of progress, as eighteenth century thought had elaborated it. In this general liberal movement it constituted a sort of left wing. It was not as certain as liberalism, either secular or religious, was that a just society could be created merely by educating men in the ideals of justice. It insisted, rather, that justice could be achieved only if the victims of injustice in society would struggle against the beneficiaries of injustice. It tried to establish contacts between the church and labor. This was true of the Christian socialist movement in the Church of England, under the leadership of men like Kingsley and Maurice. It was equally true of our American so-called "social gospel" from Rauschenbusch to the present. This radicalism was mildly socialistic. But it drew the line at revolution and disavowed the Marxian reliance upon overt social conflict. It believed that the democratic process offered a resource for social change greater than Marxians had realized. It qualified Marxism, in short, in terms of pacifism. This form of Christian radicalism became particularly authoritative in America because American liberal Protestantism was an interesting compound of the secular liberal and sectarian Christian hopes. The secular liberals believed that society was moving toward perfection. The original sectarian Christian believed that the church must obey "the law of Christ" in defiance of the world. But on the American frontier the world seemed no longer to defy "the law of Christ." A new society of liberty and equality was being built. Consequently sectarian Christians hoped for the realization of the kingdom of God on earth through a simple cooperation of the church and the world. When the sober realities of capitalism disappointed these dreams, they were only slightly remodeled and postponed. The ideal society would be established when economic life would achieve the same degree of democracy which political life had achieved. The watchword was "industrial democracy." In short, Christian socialism of the nineteenth and early twentieth century was really very similar to the ethical and utopian socialism which preceded Marx in Europe, the socialism of Saint-Simon and Fourier.

Since the war Christian socialism has changed its fundamental conceptions very radically. This change can be expressed most simply in the assertion that it has become much less critical of the political and economic analyses of Marxism and much more critical of its cultural pretensions and confusions. It inclines to agree with the Marxians that capitalism is a self-destructive economy in a technical age and that it will continue to involve itself in wars and unemployment crises. It believes this to be true because capitalism cannot establish a system of distribution in which the workers are able to buy the rough equivalent of what they produce. The consequent overproduction results in fights for foreign markets, in which surplus products can be dumped, and in domestic crises of unemployment.

The Christian Marxians also agree with orthodox Marxians that the discovery of social stupidity and the revelation of the self-destructive character of social policies does not guarantee their elimination. They do not believe that appeals to either enlightened self-interest or to moral idealism necessarily changes the policies of ruling oligarchies. They have, in other words, a rather pessimistic conception of human nature. They accept the Marxian theory of the ideological character of all moral idealism as roughly similar to the Christian idea of the sinfulness of man. They insist only that the Marxians have given the theory of ideology a much too limited interpretation. They believe that men's ideals are corrupted by their interests in general and not only by their economic interests. They point to the conflict between Stalin and Trotsky as being inexplicable in terms of the Marxian theory, which accuses only capitalists of ideological corruptions. Men in power and authority will look upon issues in which they are involved in terms other than those who are without authority and power. Christian socialists do not deny that principles may be and usually are at stake in these conflicts; but they believe that self-interest colors the purest ideals.

This tendency to carry the doctrine of determinism beyond the limits set by orthodox Marxians enables Christian socialists to be very critical toward certain aspects of Marxian politics. They believe for instance that Marxism on the whole expresses the characteristic attitudes of urban rather than agrarian workers. It has the quality of mechanistic and rationalistic thinking which characterises urban life. It has no appreciation of the unique property sense of the man of the soil and does not understand that the socialization of property cannot be carried through on the land in terms of policies borrowed from the industrial situation. Christian socialists therefore tend to believe that orthodox Marxism helps to create fascism by unnecessarily alienating agrarian and lower middle class people, who have a stronger hold on the cultural and religious inheritances of the past and whose needs are not completely met by a too simple and mechanical policy of socialization. On the other hand the modern Christian socialists do not share the hopes of Jeffersonian liberals, of whom there are a considerable number, particularly in the South, that the problem of modern civilization can be solved by decentralization, small freeholds, etc. They believe that a technical civilization makes centralization of industrial and even agrarian units of production inevitable, that collectivism is thus an established fact and that the question is: who shall control these great collectivities, irresponsible individuals or society itself?

The measure of political agreement between Christian socialists and orthodox Marxians will vary of course. In England a small group of Anglo-Catholic radicals are actually more sympathetic toward Trotsky than toward Stalin because their religious absolutism is outraged by the compromises which Stalin has made, particularly by his drift away from early equalitarian ideals. On the other hand most Christian socialists in England are in the left wing of the labor party and are generally more socialistic than the trade union leaders of the center and right. Both George Lansbury and Sir Stafford Cripps are genuine products of Christian radicalism, though they differ greatly in that Lansbury belongs to the earlier pacifistic generation while Cripps is far from being a pacifist. In America, where radical politics are not developed, Christian socialists are generally members of the socialist party though many of them have no definite political affiliation. Norman Thomas has undoubtedly received a larger percentage of votes from parsons in several elections than he received from any other professional group. The absence of any powerful socialist movement in this country does of course give a certain degree of unreality to religious socialist convictions. They are sometimes held by men who are not at all consistent in their dealing with day to day industrial issues which they confront in their several communities. On the other hand many a courageous parson is the very center of a small minority in his community, characterized on the whole by middle class complacency and political ignorance.

In regard to the cultural and religious criticisms which Christian socialists make of Marxism there are again many schools of thought. There are of course Christian socialists who identify the kingdom of God as uncritically with the "classless society" as liberals once identified it with democracy. They honestly believe that capitalism is the root of all evil. The more sophisticated Christian socialists (whose number, the writer fondly hopes, is growing), do not have such a simple explanation for human wrongdoing. They regard the disproportion of economic power in a capitalistic society as the primary root of its specific evils. But they do not believe that a socialist society would eliminate the sinfulness of man as simply as socialists expect. They are in other words rigorously opposed to the utopianism of orthodox Marxism and believe that recent events in Russia have amply justified their more realistic attitude toward human nature. They are socialists because they believe it is the duty of a Christian to affirm the highest possible justice in every society; and they regard socialism, that is the social ownership of the means of production, as a minimal requirement of social health in a technical age.

On the other hand they do not expect a socialist society to eliminate the organic cohesion of nationalities nor all the conflicts which arise from the competing will-to-power of nations. They do not expect the state to "wither away." That is, they do not take the anarchistic dreams which crown Marxian utopianism seriously. They believe that even in a socialist society there will be tendency toward friction between groups performing various functions, even if their rewards should be fairly equalized. While they regard equality as the regulative principle of justice they do not expect any society to achieve perfect equality. They believe that the mounting inequality in Russia is on the one hand the inevitable corruption of the ideal in the process of its realization. But it is on the other hand an unnecessary compromise with social forces, made by idealists who have no adequate philosophy of compromise. Equalitarians who think it is easy to introduce the principle of equality in a classless society end by sacrificing the principle beyond all recognition. Stalin needs only to denounce the ideal of equality "as a principle of Christian asceticism" to free himself for any compromise.

The Christian Marxians may not be certain that the democratic process will survive the deepest social crises unscathed. That is, they are sufficiently realistic to know that the democratic process demands the acquiescence of the minority in the will of the majority and that there are social situations in which desperate minorities will defy the majority. They do not therefore regard democracy as self-justifying. On the other hand they are deeply concerned about the problem of power in a socialist society, precisely because they are not utopians. They cannot be uncritical toward the aggrandizement of power in Russia because they are not under the illusion that the power of the state will gradually wither away. They know that the problem of power is and will always remain the crucial issue in any scheme of social justice. They want to equalize conomic power but not at the price of creating political tyranny in a socialist society. They do not trust any irresponsible power in the long run, whether it is wielded by priests, monks, capitalists or commissars.

If it be asked why Christian socialism should be so strongly opposed to utopianism the answer is that it regards utopianism as the constitutional disease of all naturalistic thought, whether liberal or radical. Naturalists regard the natural social process as self-explanatory and self-fulfilling. Thus they are opposed to every kind of supernaturalism. But the unconditioned good, which in Christian faith is the Kingdom of God, is an either explicit or implicit element in every approach to the social problem. The same naturalistic relativists, who are afraid of every transcendent reference, end by dreaming of an unconditioned social order in which perfect justice and perfect peace will be achieved. The Marxians significantly speak of a dialectical process in history which ends with the revolution. They try to make it meaningful beyond the revolution. But the dialectic process turns out to be merely between man and nature. That is, the Marxian is unable to conceive of a socialist society which might stand under the peril of an antithetical force, a new revolutionary movement. After the revolution the Marxian turns half Catholic and half liberal. He is Catholic in the sense that he tends to identify his particular institutions with the Kingdom of God as the Catholic identifies the church with it. He is liberal in that he hopes for continued progress in the socialist society but only in terms of a natural growth and not in terms of the dialectical tensions which were the very stuff of history before the revolution.

This anti-utopianism, this fear of identifying the transcendent good with the relative achievements of history, forces the Christian socialist into a qualified loyalty toward any political program. He can never regard the capitalist as the incarnation of the principle of evil, even though he does not hope with the liberal that privileged classes can be persuaded to renounce their privileges voluntarily. Nor can he ever regard one particular class as Messianic, though he may assign a very high historic mission to the industrial workers of the world.

Such religious reservations upon his political loyalties may on occasion betray the Christian socialist into political ineffectiveness. On the other hand it may increase his political wisdom. After all, every fanatic creed tends to sacrifice light for heat and to bedevil its political policies with unjustified simplifications and unnecessary hatreds. There ought therefore be a genuine place for Christian socialists in the radical movement if they affirm the general political and economic analyses and programs of socialism, even though they reject Marxism as an adequate philosophy of life. While Christian socialists are not unduly alarmed by the irreligion and anti-religion of Marxism and refuse to regard it as the primary peril of modern "Christian" civilization, they do discount this irreligion as an inheritance of the bourgeois rationalism of the eighteenth century. They think it slightly pathetic that Marxists, who pretend to defy "bourgeois ideology" on every front, should have such a touching confidence in bourgeois rationalism and naturalism as a philosophy of life. But this defect cannot be remedied by mere condemnation. Ultimately the Christian socialist must be able to prove that he can cooperate in building a better world without regarding each new political achievement as the ultimate good.

The Christian socialist believes that while some forms of revolutionary secularism may be able to express a high degree of moral tension before a revolution they are all a bad religion for a period after the revolution. For then the revolutionary ardor is transmuted into post-revolutionary complacency which accepts every dubious political compromise as a "dialectical" necessity. Of this weakness contemporary Stalinist communism is an instructive example. Nor is Trotsky convincing when he assures us that Stalin has betrayed the revolution but that it could be made to succeed if we could have only one more revolution with Trotsky as its leader.

The Christian socialist can follow neither Stalin or Trotsky. For Stalin the Kingdom of God has come. For Trotsky it is still coming. But both regard the Kingdom of God as a political possibility. The Christian socialist never expects to live in a society in which political and economic realities do not stand under the tension and the criticism of the Kingdom of God.

PART FOUR
THE NEW DEAL APPRAISED

12
THE RETROGRESSIVE ROLE OF AMERICAN LIBERALISM
V. F. Calverton*

The most unorthodox and wide-ranging American radical in the years between the World Wars may well have been Victor Francis Calverton. Born in Baltimore in 1900, he attended the Johns Hopkins University (where, he said, "I was miseducated by the professors but succeeded in educating myself by reading twelve books a week for several years."), and in 1923 founded *The Modern Quarterly,* which he edited until his death in 1940. The range of Calverton's interests was extraordinary, embracing history, literature, sociology, and anthropology; he was particularly concerned with the role of youth, women, and Negroes in America. During the late 1920's Calverton moved rather easily in communist literary circles, but in 1933 he was denounced as a "fascist" and ostracized by Party leaders for his anti-Stalinist and iconoclastic views. Nevertheless, Calverton remained a socialist who believed that Marx's insights would have to be "adapted to the American outlook." His analysis of the American liberal tradition, which appeared just before Roosevelt's first inauguration, is of particular interest. Why did Calverton believe that American liberalism, unlike its European counterpart, had played an historically retrogressive role? To what extent did sectional rivalries continue to muddle class lines in the 1930's? How valid is Calverton's assertion that liberalism had been concerned with workers not as workers but as incipient entrepreneurs? Was his critique borne out by the record of the Roosevelt administration? On this score Calverton himself had few doubts. In 1938 he concluded

*Calverton, V. F., Backward March: The Liberal Command. An Examination of the Retrogressive Role of American Liberalism, *Modern Quarterly,* VII (February, 1933), 27-32. Reprinted by permission of Lawrence and Wishart, Ltd.

that "the New Deal is an extension of old-line capitalism in new form and with a different nomenclature, and that its object is to protect capital-investment and discourage the working-class from adopting a socialist ideology." □

The time has come when American history must be revaluated and rewritten. It is only today, when certain forces in American life have reached a point of focus contributive of a clarity impossible in the past, that this revaluation can be attempted with success. In the nineteenth century the American scene was in a state which was too muddled and confused to inspire such a revaluation. At that time the interests at stake, the conflicts of purpose between classes, sections, groups, and individuals, were too blurred to be recognized clearly in terms of what they were to become. Today we can see them as the interrelated and indisseverable parts of a cultural process which is as definite and clearcut as the lines of a skyscraper.

The class lines which in the nineteenth century were so uncertain and nebulous, so bewilderingly criss-crossed and intersecting, have become clear and precise in the twentieth century. It is in the light of that new clarity that American history must be rewritten.

During the first two thirds of the nineteenth century, America was a nation created by small men, men without social station or distinction, men without means but with pluck and courage and determination, men who were individualistic-minded, democratic-spirited, and patriotic to the core. That America was animate with aspiration, impregnated with a belief in its future. When Mrs. Trollope traveled through the America of that day she was constantly annoyed by the bombardment of patriotism which greeted her on every side, in villages, towns, and cities, as also was de Tocqueville who found the Americans the most obstreperous chauvinists he had ever encountered. That patriotism, born on the rising tide of expansion of that day, penetrated throughout the length and breadth of our life. It was shared by the politicians, the literati, the well-to-do, and the populace on the street. It was in the writing of American history, symbolized in the work of Bancroft, that that spirit became most unrestrained and vociferous. In the eyes of Bancroft, for example, everything American was sacred; everything this country ever attempted was right; from the founders of the country to the leaders of that day no blemish was to be noted, so noble had been their intentions and so fruitfully had they been fulfilled. Like the cherry-tree Washington of Weems' biography, the country and its leaders were sheathed in a mist of fabled rectitude and virtue.

As long as the country remained in its expanding stage, that tendency of interpretation continued to dominate the spirit of American history. When the twentieth century arrived, however, and the days of expansion were over, and the small man found himself being beaten over the head by the big man in the field of business as well as agriculture, that tendency ceased. Since that time the halo which once enshrouded American institutions and leaders has disappeared. Beginning with the era of the muckrakers things American began to look exceedingly sick and shoddy. With the advance of liberal scholarship, an outgrowth of the muckraking decade and of the spirit of defeat which had come upon the land with the defeat of the small man on the economic field, the American scene was subjected to a new interpretation. Exposing as it did the monetary machinations behind many of our most lauded achievements, the liberal tradition encouraged the tendency to scoff and sneer at American traditions. It was out of that tendency that the "debunkers" of American history sprang. The achievements of the Revolutionary War were debunked; the importance of the Civil War was debunked; the pertinence and place of various individuals in the historical process were debunked–in fact, everything was debunked with an indiscriminate enthusiasm which betrayed the lack of historical insight involved in the whole approach. Instead of seeing the development of America as part of its progressive advance as a historic whole, and evaluating its phenomena and its leaders in relationship with that development, the debunkers adjudge everything and everybody in reference to the immediate criteria of today, stressing with a narrow-mindedness culpably characteristic of defeatist historians the corruption involved in the *means* but neglecting entirely the significance involved in the *ends*. It is easy to attack the motivations behind many of the leaders in the Revolutionary War or the Civil War or the Reconstruction period, but it is a much more difficult and valuable task to determine the significance of those events in relationship to the historic advance of the country as a unit.

The great problem confronting and challenging us today, therefore, is not that of debunking our past but of revaluating it in terms of our revolutionary tradition. In a word, we must learn not to scoff at our revolutionary past but to build upon it.

What we must see is that in every phase of our development there have been progressive as well as reactionary forces at work, and if the progressive forces of one day lose their progressiveness in the next that is no reason why we should disregard the important influence which they exerted at the time they were progressive. What we must do is to evaluate every period in terms of the forces active at the time, differentiating those that were progressive from those that were retrogressive, showing in just what ways those that were progressive tended to shape the developments in our society which are important to understanding its character today and its possibilities of change tomorrow.

By employing that approach, it can be seen at once that things American must be adjudged by different standards than things European, since American social and economic conditions have been so different from those present in Europe. American history is usually misjudged because of the neglect of that difference. In discussing the theme of this article, for example, it can be said at once that if we mean by a revolution what the French Revolution of 1789 signifies or the Bolshevik Revolution of 1917, then America has had no revolutionary history at all. What is necessary to stress at this point, in keeping with our previous observations, is that America has evolved differently from European countries, creating a different cultural pattern in the process, and developing a different series of social struggles with different revolutionary implications. It is those differences which must be understood first if there is to be any appreciation of the significance and challenge of our revolutionary history.

In Europe the great social struggles of the seventeenth, eighteenth, and early nineteenth centuries were those fought between the landed aristocracies and the commercial and industrial bourgeoisie. In America those struggles took on an entirely different character. The earliest approach to a landed aristocracy that America ever had was in the patroon system and the vast landed estates which had been dealt out by English kings as special grants to various individuals who stood high in royal favor. But that landed aristocracy, largely Tory in extraction, which, due to the rapid rise in power of the merchant class, had never been able to function effectively, disappeared with the close of the Revolutionary War. Its representatives or defendants, Tories in the main, were driven out by force by the bourgeoisie who were the patriots of the period. The Revolutionary War, then, was a progressive war in that it dealt the first death-blow to American feudalism. After the Revolutionary War, the only remnant of feudalism which persisted was the presence of the plantation aristocracy in the South. The struggle between the North and the South which developed with violent intensity during the first half of the nineteenth century, reaching its climax in the Civil War, marked the last conflict between the landed aristocracy and the bourgeoisie in the nation. The Civil War meted out the final death blow to feudal institutions in this country. After the Civil War, the class struggle in America changed character and became a conflict between the upper bourgeoisie and the petty bourgeoisie, big business and small business, with the growing proletariat of the time allying itself politically with the cause of the latter. The landed class disappeared as a separate social force and became absorbed into the maw of the commercial and industrial structure. Big business in the form of the banks, the loan associations, and the railroads, sunk its tentacles into the land, mortgaging it beyond redemption. The small farmer and the small business man found themselves face to face with the same foe, big business in the guise of the financier and the industrialist. The struggle between those two forces absorbed the *revolutionary* energy, of the American people throughout the nineteenth century and in decreasing degree continues to do so even today.

Now the very fact that the struggle against feudalism in America assumed in the Civil War the form of a sectional conflict instead of a national conflict of classes, thwarted the development of a revolutionary ideology on the part of the bourgeois forces which were bent upon the destruction of the feudal way of life. *In all European countries, for example, the battle which the bourgeoisie carried on against feudalism led to the creation of a revolutionary ideology which found dynamic expression in economics, politics, religion, and ethics.* Freedom of speech, press, religion, became the great rallying cries of the revolutionary bourgeoisie in Europe. The struggle for the right to economic freedom, that is freedom for the middle class from the restrictions of the aristocracy, lent the cause of the European bourgeoisie a fierce fighting character, which found its summation in the liberal idealism of the eighteenth and nineteenth centuries. The fact that that conflict followed sectional instead of national class lines in this country robbed us of that heritage of progressive liberal idealism, *and twisted and distorted our whole political outlook in such ways that class interests became blurred by sectional prejudices, with antagonistic classes resolving their conflicts with each other (which under different conditions would have led them to open strife) into a mutual alliance against their accepted sectional foe.* Even today the South provides a clear-cut example of the confusing consequences of that alliance. Active as various aspects of the class struggle are in the South today, the South as a whole, proletarians as well as sharecroppers, poor whites as well as successful bourgeoisie, stand politically as one in their uncompromising support of the Democratic party. (Only the religious issue in the preceding election could in any way shake the strength and solidity of that union.) In short, their sectional hostility to the North, derivative from the struggle between the two sections in the Civil War, is still greater than their class hostility to each other. This sectional fact has definitely held back the development of a nation-wide revolutionary outlook along class lines in this country.

Paradoxically enough, because of the factors we have stressed, *liberalism has been forced to play an economically retrogressive instead of progressive rôle in American life.* The progressive liberal tradition developed by the bourgeoisie in England, for example, sprang out of its fight against the aristocracy and the necessity of destroying the feudal way of life. The so-called liberal tradition in America, on the other hand, developed as a definite defense against the advancing bourgeois way of life. Its energies were wasted in a futile attempt to hold back the progressive development of capitalist enterprise.

In European countries liberalism derived its fighting vigor from the intensity of its conflict with the landed class. Its revolutionary fight for its various freedoms, freedom of speech, freedom of press, freedom before the law, lent its cause a challenging progressive character, for it was those freedoms which were necessary to the advance of middle class society at that time. Moreover, its whole philosophy became identified with the advancing forms of bourgeois enterprise. In this country, on the other hand, as we noted before, the reverse occurred. Liberalism in America became identified with the retrogressive instead of progressive forms of bourgeois enterprise, and hence developed a backward instead of forward looking philosophy of life. Without appreciating the significance of that difference, it is impossible to understand the singular development of American political and social thought.

Beginning with Jefferson, American liberalism favored agrarianism as opposed to industrialism and fought the introduction of manufactures into American life; it advocated decentralization instead of centralization of government and enterprise, with the result that it defended competition as the basis of progress and attacked all forms of corporate organization and control. Aiming to preserve competition instead of to destroy it, it devoted its energies to retarding the progressive rôle that big business, by the very nature of its objectives, was scheduled to perform, namely, to eliminate competition within the respective industries by the organization of corporations, trusts, and monopolies to take the place of the myriad-fold competing enterprises and proprietors.*

In brief, American liberalism from the very start was reactionary in that it defended competition instead of opposing it, thereby helping to hold back the progressive advance of our economic life. Sentimentally, to be sure, it stood up for the cause of the individual, defending his rights against those of big business and the centralized state; realistically, however, it fought to preserve a way of life which early in the nineteenth century had begun to become retrogressive. It defended the interests of the small farmer and the small business man against those of the large capitalist and financier, although it was the large capitalist and financier, the Rockefellers, the Carnegies, the Morgans, who were to make possible the reorganization of our economic life in such ways as to prepare the groundwork for a more cooperative world wherein competition would not exist and individualism would disappear. It was in that sense that American liberalism was retrogressive instead of progressive in its outlook. It was as capitalistic in its logic as big business, save that it wanted capitalism to proceed on a small scale instead of a vast, concentrated one. It wanted a world which was filled with predatory wolves and foxes but in which there were no all-powerful lions. What it did not see was that it was the lions, though at the cost of life of the smaller animals, who brought order out of chaos, lifting the world in which they lived from a lower to a higher state of existence.

Indeed, we can say at this point that the whole development of revolutionary thought in this country has been impeded and distorted by the retrogressive character of American liberalism. In the early conflict between Jefferson and Hamilton, for instance, it was the conservative Hamilton who was right in his emphasis upon the importance of encouraging industries and in his advocacy of a sound national finance, while it was the liberal Jefferson who was wrong in his hostility to

---

*It is important here to observe that while big business tended to engulf the small proprietor, and thus destroy competition within the individual industry, it did not tend of itself to destroy competition between the large industries, corporations, or trusts. Nor did it tend to destroy competition on the international field; in fact, in many ways it tended to accentuate it there. John D. Rockefeller, for instance, practically eliminated all competition from the oil fields in this country, but that did not mean that he eliminated competition on the international field. On the contrary, it made international competition, as between Standard Oil and Royal Dutch Shell, a matter of much graver import, with warlike implications writ large in its structure.

industries and in his opposition to every form of national control. A century later, American liberalism was guilty of the same fallacy. Bryan had not advanced a step beyond Jefferson in his economic philosophy, except that he did not attack the development of industries,–industries having grown by that time to so large a stature that the only thing possible to attack were their tendencies toward expansion.

In fact the whole history of American liberalism stretching from Jefferson to Bryan, and then down to Wilson and LaFollette, did nothing more than comprise new and ever more pathetic testimonies of the futile, economically backward character of the liberal cause. Industrialism having planted itself ineradicably in our soil, Jefferson's stand on the question could no longer be defended. But the attempt of the later liberals to restrain the development of industry was essentially no less retrogressive an influence. Woodrow Wilson's platitudes about "the new freedom" were no more sound or progressive than Theodore Roosevelt's Billy Sundaylike denunciations of the trusts, or LaFollette's infantile proposals that we return to the days of 1776. Franklin D. Roosevelt's voluble promises to restore power to the "forgotten man" retain the same anachronistic echo. Without exception, then, American liberalism, changing though it did with new conditions, has continued throughout our history to play a retarding rôle in our economic life. However much it altered its program, under the pressure of changing social forces, it constantly remained, from the days of Jefferson to those of Wilson, backward-gazing in its economic outlook. Caught in the beginning by environment and a philosophy which were predominantly agrarian, it became handicapped almost at birth with an economic myopia which eventually proved to be an immedicable affliction. Because of the affliction, it was the conservatives in America, paradoxical as it may seem, who were progressive in economic vision and the liberals who were retrogressive. Hamilton was economically more progressive than Jefferson at the end of the eighteenth century, and the Republican party was economically more progressive than the Democratic at the end of the nineteenth. Today neither party has a progressive economic rôle to perform. Both are equally retrogressive. Progress now lies in a new, collectivistic direction which only a radical proletarian party can convert into a program of action.

It is only by understanding the backward rôle which American liberalism has played in our history that we can understand the pathetic lack of social clarity in the philosophies of such outstanding American "progressives" as John Dewey, William Graham Sumner, Charles A. Beard, James Harvey Robinson, Frederick C. Howe, Herbert Croly, Jane Addams,

Walter Weyl, Lincoln Steffens, Harry Elmer Barnes, and others, and realize why America has created no sociological school of consequence. Enamored of the backward looking philosophy of American liberalism, with its emphases upon agrarian democracy and equality and upon individualism and the inspiration of the competitive drive, these so-called progressives expended their ardor and energy in fighting futile battles with an enemy that grew stronger with every attack they hazarded against it. Lilliputian zealots advancing upon a Brobdignagian foe, their tragic struggle seems almost comic in present-day perspective. Lacking the strength which communicates itself to those allied to a progressive cause, they were never able to endow their liberalism with the insight and intelligence which characterized European liberalism at its heyday of development.

The only progressive influence that American liberalism ever exercised was in providing early in the nineteenth century the necessary incentive and inspiration to encourage the masses to go West and populate the country, but even that influence behaved like a boomerang once the migrations were in full swing, for its immediate political impact was to combat the rise of industry and defend the cause of agriculture. Indeed, the land issue assumed such a commanding aspect that even when a liberal thinker acquired a degree of social-mindedness he tended to go off on a tangent like Henry George with his lopsided emphasis upon the panacea-like qualities of the Single Tax. But it was that same land factor with its individualistic challenge which also misled the others, tending to make them believe, one in this way, one in another, that the individual and not society was the center of things, and that reform to possess significance must be dedicated to a defense of individual interests even at the cost of those of society. Identified with the small agrarianite on one side and the small urbanite on the other, it was inevitable that their logic should be retrogressive in emphasis. The democracy they were interested in was not the industrial or proletarian democracy of the modern radical but the democracy of the small farmer and the small business man and entrepreneur in the cities. In a word, they were not interested in proletarians as proletarians, but in proletarians as potential bourgeois. They were determined to think of American society as a classless phenomenon, uncognizant that what they were doing was supporting the middle class, first as agrarianites and later on as urbanites as well, with its futile stress upon an individualistic economic outlook which had been rendered anachronistic by the technical processes of production and social organization.

It was in the twentieth century that liberal thought in America became most dangerously retrogressive. By virtue of its false promises and compelling rhetoric it was able to conceal from the minds of millions of Americans the existence of certain ineradicable fundamentals. In the form of the platitude-mongering Wilson, who was willing to have young men die for old men's dividends, while he spread peace over the no-man's land of posterity, liberalism cashed in on its thirty pieces of silver and crucified itself on the wrong cross. It thought that it was Jesus but found out when it was too late that it was Judas in disguise. By talking about love of humanity instead of trying to discover how to create it, it succeeded only in spreading more hate and horror in a world that was already stinking with it from every nostril, buttock, and mouth. But Wilson's folly was not singular. It was the product of his generation, of the whole liberal way of thought. Before the War it had been in the educational philosophy of John Dewey, in the mystic nationalism of Herbert Croly, and in the pacifism of Jane Addams.

Products of the ideology of the lower middle class, they couldn't see the fundamentals involved in all issues which they discussed. Wilson couldn't see that a League of Nations can't function in a capitalist world; and Dewey couldn't see that democracy in education cannot prevail in a plutocracy and that vocationalized education in our system of society is but another way of perpetuating the prevailing plutocracy—any more than Charles Beard today, still a votary of the liberal tradition, can see that economic planning cannot be successful in an economic system which continues to defend private property and the profit motivation.

Although the American liberalism of the nineteenth century is dead, as well as that derivative of the Wilsonian tradition, twentieth century post-war liberalism has one more retrogressive function to perform, namely, to abet the rise of an American fascism which will ultimately repudiate everything which the liberal tradition once stood for—but which the liberals will believe is liberal still.

13
THE ROOSEVELT EXPERIMENT
Harold Laski*

From the time of Alexis de Tocqueville, some of the keenest observers of the American experience have been foreign visitors. Using Europe as a point of reference they have often acquired unusual insight into American social and political institutions. This was surely true of Harold Laski, the noted political scientist and advisor to the British Labour Party, who brought to his analysis of the New Deal not only a European perspective but a socialist one as well. Unlike Tocqueville, who studied the United States in the belief that Europe would follow in the path of egalitarian democracy, Laski studied the United States in the expectation that it would ultimately move in the direction of welfare-state collectivism. One theme of his last book, *The American Democracy* (1948), was that a continuing commitment to outworn individualistic values interfered with the socialist organization of economy required by modern industrialism. Yet early in the 1930's Laski had been somewhat more sanguine. His evaluation of the New Deal's prospects in 1934 illustrates the enthusiasm Franklin Roosevelt kindled among European socialists; it expresses as well their concurrent fear that hostile forces would block the New Deal in mid-channel. Moreover, his article raises a number of relevant questions. Is there any contradiction between his assertion that the New Deal derived logically from the Progressive movement yet was based on a "sober conservatism"? Does his interpretation of the American liberal tradition differ in any important respect from that of Calverton? How realistic is Laski's argument that the price of New Deal success would have to be the voluntary abdication of the capitalist class? Which forces does he believe were moving in Roosevelt's favor, and which were not? □

I

Russia apart, no modern state has undertaken an experiment which even approaches in magnitude or significance the adventure upon which

---

*Laski, Harold J., The Roosevelt Experiment, *The Atlantic Monthly,* **CLIII** (February, 1934), 143-53. Reprinted by permission of *The Atlantic Monthly.*

President Roosevelt has embarked. There have been attempts to regulate the hours and wages of particular persons in particular industries. There have been important schemes of social legislation, like the British system of unemployment insurance. War-time necessity has induced the limitation of profit for a special period, and certain vital industries have sometimes, either permanently or for a period, come under the direct ownership and control of a public authority. There has even, as in the Germany of the post-war epoch, been a partnership, though indirect, between industry and the state.

But President Roosevelt is the first statesman in a great capitalist society who has sought deliberately and systematically to use the power of the state to subordinate the primary assumptions of that society to certain vital social purposes. He is the first statesman deliberately to experiment on a wholesale scale with the limitation of the profit-making motive. He is the first statesman, again in a wholesale way, to attack not the secondary but the primary manifestations of the doctrine of *laissez faire*. He is the first statesman who, of his own volition, and without coercion, either direct or indirect, has placed in the hands of organized labor a weapon which, if it be used successfully, is bound to result in a vital readjustment of the relative bargaining power of Capital and Labor. He is also the first statesman who, the taxing power apart, has sought to use the political authority of the state to compel, over the whole area of economic effort, a significant readjustment of the national income.

No unbiased spectator of the adventure involved can withhold his admiration for the courage such an effort has implied. Success or failure, it bears upon its face the hallmarks of great leadership. Improvised in haste, devised under the grim pressure of crisis, imposed, as no doubt it has been imposed, in an atmosphere of panic and bewilderment, it stands out in remarkable, even significant, contrast to the economic policy of any other capitalist government in the world. Compared, for example, with the unimaginative activity of the British Government,–which rode to power on a wave of kindred enthusiasm,–it is an exhilarating spectacle. Great Britain has simply sought to lend the aid of government to the ancient technique of capitalist enterprise; it has had no sense that what is in question is the very foundations of that system. President Roosevelt has, in effect, challenged American capitalism to coöperate with him in transforming itself into a social experiment. And in doing so he has displayed, granted the conditions he confronts, a creative audacity, a sense of psychological essentials, an eye for the pivotal matters involved, which deserve well of the commonwealth he seeks to serve. Russia again apart, there has been no adventure of comparable range of intensity in modern times.

II

But it is one thing to plan boldly; it is another, and a very different thing, to plan successfully. Before we can judge the effort upon which Mr. Roosevelt is engaged, it is necessary to know what the implications of his adventure actually are, and the relation of these to the total social situation in which he finds himself involved. For it is dangerous to experiment with the foundations of a society unless the experiment be built upon doctrinal assumptions the conclusions of which follow with irresistible logic from the premises it is legitimate to use.

Mr. Roosevelt is not, as it were, merely in the position of an engineer who is erecting bulwarks against a temporary and unexpected flood. His experiment, no doubt, happens to coincide with the onset of economic disaster; but he is driven, by its profundity, not only to dissipate its effects, but also to lay the foundations of a new social order from which, so far as human prescience can avail, such disasters have been banished. What, therefore, is important in the estimate of his effort is not merely the objectives he has set before himself, but the spirit and temper of the setting those objectives encounter. He is attempting a revolution by consent; and it is the latter term in his equation that is fundamental to the formation of a judgment.

For the actual objectives themselves are not matters a reasonable observer can seriously dispute. The America he took over in March of 1933 was in a highly dangerous condition. It was not merely that there were some fourteen millions of unemployed, largely dependent upon a casual charity which was breaking down. It was not merely that, among the employed themselves, short time was dangerously widespread. It was not merely, either, that wages had been reduced during the depression in a fashion rivaled only by the desperate experiments of Dr. Bruening in Germany. It was not merely, again, that the whole banking structure of the United States was cracking and that, with the largest gold reserve in the history of the world, the foundations of her currency system were completely insecure. Even more urgent were two other facts.

The American people, dazed by the width and intensity of the crisis, had lost confidence in the *bona fides* of the system under which they lived. Its principles seemed to them dubious, and they were prepared for a challenge to its values. The remedies, moreover, which the President had to apply needed application in an era of profound technological revolution, on the one hand, and insane economic nationalism on the other. At a time, that is, when the popular test of Mr. Roosevelt's policies would necessarily be his success in absorbing the unemployed into work, scientific discovery and organization had made possible increasing production with an ever-decreasing working force, while each nation-state, confronted as it was with kindred problems of its own, was seeking by tariffs and quotas, embargoes and currency restrictions, to impede the recovery of international trade.

He was, moreover, at work in an epoch of grave political crisis. The failure of disarmament, the menace of Japanese imperialism, the arrival of Herr Hitler in power, continuous disturbance in South America, and a Southeastern Europe given over to bitter repression—all these made for an insecurity which endangered the psychological conditions of economic advance. He had to fight for the growth of American markets abroad in an atmosphere unfavorable to the very notion of commerce. He was battling for the confidence which precedes revival when the League of Nations was being struck blow after blow, and the prospect of Europe seemed more akin to that of the years immediately preceding the war than at any time since the Armistice of 1918. In Europe and the Far East, in fact, force and unreason dominated the minds of men. Traditional values were in the melting pot; and, as in all epochs where basic changes are under discussion, panic and doubt and even persecution prevented any calm estimation of the effort Mr. Roosevelt had undertaken.

III

Men have spoken easily of his radicalism. Yet, so far as his politics have revealed themselves, what will strike the observer is less their radicalism, currency apart, than the sober conservatism upon which they have been built.

The Securities Act has aroused passionate indignation. Yet the sober critic who analyzes its clauses with detachment will take a very different view. He will point out that it is built upon the solid experience, now extending over a generation, of British company law; that it meets the conditions first revealed by Mr. Justice Brandeis over twenty years ago; that there is no technique within its interstices not amply justified by the

Senate revelations of corporation practice in recent years. The striking thing about the Securities Act is not its practically unanimous passage. The striking thing is that the United States should have had to wait until 1933 before legislative sanction was given to the most elementary precautions required by the investor under modern conditions. No serious student of the Securities Act but will be tempted to conclude that it could only be opposed by men who have something to conceal; and if he looks through the pages of the testimony before the Senate he will amply understand the indignation of opponents. It is the prohibition of obvious malpractice which always awakens the loudest clamor from its exponents.

Nor can the National Recovery Act be held to involve any striking innovations. Stripped of its resounding terminology, it merely gives effect to ideas which have been the commonplace of economic discussion these thirty years. The abolition of child labor puts an end to what has been too long an indefensible stain upon American social conditions; it terminates a form of slavery for which no defense in principle is possible. The codes–none of which is radical in essence–merely give national status to the regulation of hours and wages which, even in America, have been the object of successful experiment ever since the famous Oregon Statute of 1903 and the Adamson Law of 1917; their substance has been consecrated piecemeal not merely by so eminently conservative a body as the Supreme Court,–by which it may be taken as proved that they represent the accepted mental climate of social well-being,–but by the preponderant opinion of economists all over the world. In principle, they are nothing more than the British system of trade boards against sweating in industry; and the wonder is that men can still be found to inspect their well-tried habits in a mood of panic.

More important, of course, are the clauses which open the door to trade-union recognition. Here one need not doubt that the prospect emerges of a wide invasion of traditional industrial practice. American trade-unionism has neither the stability nor the profundity of its British analogue. The persistence of that individualism which still lingers on from the habits of a frontier psychology has hardly domesticated it as a normal part of American life. Yet the foreigner who remembers the conditions in the coal fields of Illinois, or the steel mills of Pittsburgh, or who realizes the social gain in human welfare which has resulted from the work of Sidney Hillman in the garment trades, will have no difficulty in understanding why Mr. Justice Holmes could insist, in *Coppage* v. *Kansas,* that liberty of contract only begins where equality of bargaining power begins; his wonder, as with the Securities Act, will rather be that giant organization of American industry has not long ago resulted in an American trade-unionism more equal in intensity to the masses which require its protection. More than that; he will not find it easy to understand how industrialists like Mr. Ford can still delude themselves with the belief that rational economic relations can develop in a society like America if the individual contract is to be the basis upon which its structure is to be founded.

Nor is the situation different when one turns to other aspects of the field. A national policy of public works is not, it is true, one of those principles of economic policy upon which expert opinion is finally agreed; but it may be said without undue exaggeration that the consensus of expert opinion is definitely on the side of wise spending. In this aspect, the battle is transferred from the plane of principle to that of its wise application; and the subject matter of dispute then becomes less an embarkation upon this policy than a question as to whether Mr. Ickes and his colleagues can discover undeniable objects of beneficent expenditure.

So, too, in the field of credits and relief to those staggering under the burden of mortgage. Of the first it may be briefly said that it differs only from well-proved experiments in the past by reason of the extent of the commitments undertaken; it will appear commonplace and uninteresting if America emerges successfully from the present crisis. And of the second it may be said with emphasis that a government which, in a period of rigorous deflation, failed to assist its primary producers with legislation intended to secure relief from the pressure of mortgages would have invited the onset of a revolutionary temper. Only the mystic can tell whether order is heaven's first law; but certainly the preservation of its elementary conditions is the obvious duty of a government which is concerned for the preservation of the peace. . . .

IV

So regarded, the purposes which underlie the Roosevelt experiment constitute a perfectly intelligible whole. They are not entirely born, and it is important to realize that they have not been entirely born, from the disasters of the last four years, though these, no doubt, have lent them their emotional intensity. They go back, as purposes, to the Progressive movement of the first years of this century; and, seen in proper perspective, they are simply a development of that revolt and of the

Wilsonian legislation (notably of the Federal Reserve Act) which represents its earlier culmination. They represent a profound wave of half-articulate protest against the character of contemporary American capitalism. They represent the profound sense that what were proclaimed as its excrescences had in fact become parts of its essential nature. They express the realization that the centralization of financial power in Wall Street had become incompatible with the public well-being, especially when Wall Street had shown itself so incapable of distinguishing between that well-being and its private interests as the Senate revelations had made obvious. They express the demand, first, that American industry and finance shall operate only under a code of behavior which makes public well-being a major factor in the policies they pursue, and, second, that the government of the United States shall, as the agent of the citizens, be powerful enough to enforce the observance of that code upon all to whom it applies.

The Roosevelt experiment, in a word, is a systematic effort to put capitalism into leading strings of principle. It is to be the servant, and not the master, of the American people. For any other relationship is held, on experience, to be incompatible with ordered social progress.

There is nothing revolutionary or even novel in all this; it is worth remembering that de Tocqueville, nearly a century ago, warned America how dangerous was its alternative. It is inevitable, sooner or later, in any society built upon universal suffrage that the people should use its political power to mitigate the consequences of unrestricted capitalism; and severe disaster, like that which has characterized the last four years, only stimulates that temper more intensely. For it cannot be too often insisted, as Mr. Keynes has so often emphasized, that capitalism, by the law of its psychological being, needs to be immensely more successful than any alternative economic arrangement if it is to retain the allegiance of a multitude which possesses political power. The disparities of its results are too irrational for any alternative attitude to be possible over any long space of time. And the changed temper was made the more inevitable by the crude optimism of its defenders in the era of Coolidge and Hoover. They had raised the expectations of the multitude to such dizzy heights that their failure to satisfy them was bound to result in a scrutiny of foundations.

We must not forget that the election of 1932 was the expression of nothing so much as a demand for this scrutiny by angry and bewildered men who had entered the Promised Land only to discover that it was a desert. In dealing with their discontent, President Roosevelt has shown high qualities of enterprise and courage; but those who doubt the wisdom of his effort ought to remember that unless he had shown those qualities the patience of the multitude would have been brought to breaking point. He is not a revolutionist pursuing some private Utopia by the light of an inner wisdom. He is the logical expression of social forces and could hardly have acted otherwise if he wished to retain the characteristic contours of American life.

The remarkable thing about his innovations is not their size, but the immediacy of their relation to the traditional liberalism of America. It is the vigor with which they have been uttered, the coherence which has, as a problem in time, projected them upon a single plane, which have led men to signalize them as the herald of a new day. Yet, even if they wholly succeed, no radical would be tempted to regard them as anything more than a necessary historic phase in the slow evolution of American capitalism. They spring, at every turn, from the obvious experience of events.

V

What is likely to be their fate? In the first days of office Mr. Roosevelt had behind him a united opinion such as America appears hardly to have known. Opposition seemed less silent than dead. The activity at Washington was so intense that men seemed clearly to feel that they had entered a new epoch of American history. The American people had come into its own. The unemployed were to be halved in numbers by the autumn. The price level was to be raised to that of 1926; the primary producer was to be safeguarded; the wage earner was to have a new standard of life under conditions more equitably related to the new economic possibilities. The verve and spirit of the adventure seemed, at the outset, powerful enough to breast all obstacles it might encounter.

Nor has the opposition, even nine months after the adventure was begun, ventured into the open. It has preferred to proceed by indirection rather than by frontal attack. It does not coöperate; it mutters its doubts; it hints at the hesitation of the 'sound' men before the possibilities of a cataclysm. Mr. Roosevelt is headed for inflation; he is pledging government credit dangerously; he is spending in a reckless fashion for which there is no justification. The Securities Act is a discouragement to the legitimate activities of the Stock Exchange. The National Recovery Act is a Bolshevik interference with the rights of property, an 'un-American' attack upon a tried and tested individualist system. Wall Street is confident that traditional America is being handed over to wild professors with no regard for the practical limits to government action. It suffers from an 'emotional paralysis' when it sees its accepted canons disregarded. It floats no new issues; it resents the attacks upon its leading men. Among the great figures of American business there has been something which can only be called a psychological sabotage. They are asked to enter a new world the principles of which seem to them a clear contradiction of their historic experience of economic function. They cannot believe in the success of the adventure. They await, a little anxiously, its failure.

A 'sound' policy they would be prepared to support. Revival depends, they argue, on business men being assured of the ability to sell at a profit. Of this the conditions are well known. There must be drastic deflation; there must be reduced governmental expenditures so that lower taxation may encourage enterprise; wages must be cut to suit the new low level of prices; subsidies to industry, as with the tragic tenderness of Mr. Roosevelt for the farmer, must be abandoned; business must be left to deal with its employees in its own way; and there must be an assurance, as near absolute as may be, of a sound dollar. When these things come, the present uncertainties will disappear; men will recognize the familiar landmarks of approaching prosperity. Given their advent, Mr. Roosevelt may look to the business community for all the coöperation necessary to tide over the crisis.

It is familiar doctrine. It is the gospel of Coolidge and Hoover. It is also the gospel which produced the disaster out of which Mr. Roosevelt emerged as President. If his election meant anything at all, it was a repudiation of that gospel by the common people of America. Had he embraced it, with the terrible social losses its application involves, it is difficult to see how America could have passed through the last nine months without a major drift toward a revolutionary condition. He has retained the confidence of the people in the existing order because they really believed him when he said that they were to be given a 'new deal.' By that faith only was he able to preserve peace. Had he trodden the traditional path, he would have produced, by the costs involved, a state of rebellion among innumerable citizens who normally ask nothing better than to remain enfolded in their private lives.

He has convinced these men of his good faith. But he has not convinced the business community. They doubt his principles; they resent profoundly the intense effort he has made to compel them to abdicate from an authority which has not hitherto been seriously challenged in American history. And it is just here, it may be argued, that the crux of the Roosevelt experiment lies. Business men and financiers will not seriously be won to Mr. Roosevelt's programme until its success is proved by the return of prosperity; and prosperity is unlikely to return unless he can win the support of the financiers and business men. This is the dilemma the administration confronts; and only as it is to be met can we measure the implications of the time.

VI

The situation, says Mr. Lippmann, who has an exceptional access to the mind of Wall Street, demands 'a loyal determination to attain the objects of the reforms, sincere resolution to maintain the new standards of financial practice.' But the object of the reforms is no less a thing than to destroy the unlimited power of American capitalism to shape the contours of American life. It is to end the unbridled individualism of Mr. Ford; it is to break in pieces the industrial feudalism of the barons of coal and steel. To 'maintain the new standards of financial practice' is to ask the banker and the broker not merely to remake habits which, by their present sabotage, they clearly regard as legitimate; it is also to ask them to subordinate themselves to new purposes which they seem to consider incompatible with that profit-making motive which is the law of their being. What are the prospects of so formidable a demand?

Let us put this in another way. The men to whom Mr. Roosevelt is appealing have no serious doubts of the existing order. They made it and control it; they look upon their handiwork and declare it to be in general substance good. Mr. Roosevelt, in effect, asks them to abdicate from their control. He seeks to socialize the profit-making motive by making its operation subordinate to a body of ethical principles from which their practice has been wholly alien. They have no conviction that these principles are wise and good. They realize that their supremacy is threatened. They feel that it is challenged not merely by men of whose expertness they are unconvinced, but for ends which have never been tried. They deeply resent the speed with which they are called upon to adjust themselves to a new mental climate. They have not only the fear which comes from experience of an insecure world; they have also the indignation which accompanies any challenge which is, as explicitly as this, a denial of their title to supremacy. To be the servants of the government instead of its masters, to live by principle instead of making it, these seem to them something like a denial of the law of their being. And when all this is added to a general skepticism of all the ends Mr. Roosevelt is seeking to serve, not less than doubt of the means by which he is seeking to attain them, it is easy to understand why the 'loyal determination' of which Mr. Lippmann speaks is a far harder thing to accomplish than he seems to imagine.

How hard it is there is endless evidence to prove. It is not merely shown in individual acts of resistance like that of Mr. Ford, or in the grim conflicts which have been waged against the miners who seek to take advantage of the code and assert their right to trade-unions. It is shown not merely when the mayor of a steel town can deny a cabinet minister the right of freedom of speech. . . . It is shown, above all, in what a great financial journal terms the 'emotional paralysis' of Wall Street—perhaps the happiest euphemism for sabotage in the history of the language. For when the success or failure of Mr. Roosevelt's effort turns upon the reopening of the capital markets, those who refuse the risk of attempting their reopening are, in fact, securing the certainty of its failure. For if the market remains closed, Mr. Roosevelt has no alternative but inflation; and he is then confronted by two roads either of which leads inevitably to confusion and disaster.

To the outsider, therefore, it appears not unreasonable to argue that the absence of the 'loyal' coöperation which Mr. Lippmann so earnestly desires is not so very difficult to explain. Men who reject a new faith—for the 'New Deal' *is* a new faith—do not enter into communion with its votaries by persuasion. Historically, it has never been the habit of a class voluntarily to abdicate from power. That has always been accomplished, as in 1789 in France, or in 1917 in Russia, by violence; or, as in England in 1832, by the threat of violence the success of which was overwhelmingly probable.

The old industrial feudalism does not believe that its day is dead. It recognizes, a little sadly, the emotional success of the new religion; but it calculates, not without reason, that the new religion, to secure objective establishment, must prove itself by the miracles it can perform. It realizes that it has the key to miracles in its own hands; and it sees no reason why it should surrender the key. It has seen new faiths before—Bryan in 1896, Roosevelt in 1912. In the end they have always been defeated; and industrial feudalism has returned—as it conceives, unimpaired in strength—to the enjoyment of its empire.

It is a calculation far from devoid of substance. To maintain his hold of the popular mind Mr. Roosevelt must have a rapid success. He cannot keep Congress in a mood of subservience through 1934; and there is then a new election with all the hope a new election implies. The Supreme Court may not share the exaltation of his mood; a blow from the Supreme Court would seem a vital vindication of Congressional skepticism. Foreign opinion is largely hostile or suspicious, at least in the right circles; and, properly reported in the United States, it may create those winds of doctrine from which the old, solid Republicanism may arise purified and refreshed.

The constant flux of advisory influences at Washington is suggestive of at least the possibility that Mr. Roosevelt himself is devoid of certainty; and a high priest who doubts his own creed does not permanently convince his followers. When to these prospects is added the natural resentment of the financiers at their exclusion from a White House which, save for the intervals of Cleveland and Wilson, they have been accustomed at least since the Civil War to think of as an annex to Wall Street, it does not become difficult to understand the psychological considerations which tempt big business to assume that time is on its side.

'It is for Wall Street to decide,' writes Mr. Lippmann, 'whether in principle it will accept the "New Deal" or resist it.' Those are significant words. They assume a right in Wall Street to decide whether to wreck an experiment in which public opinion is whole-heartedly on the side of the President; on which, also, the whole future of the United States decidedly depends. Even a relatively detached observer like Mr. Lippmann can assume without discussion that Wall Street has a choice; he does not think it necessary to discuss whether Wall Street is not also under an obligation to accept the emphatic will of the American people. If that discussion does not appear necessary to Mr. Lippmann, it is reasonable to assume that it does not appear necessary in Wall Street. Once that can be said, it may be argued with conviction that Wall Street will not lightly coöperate in the surrender of its kingdom.

VII

So, as it seems, the issue is joined. The adventure upon which Mr. Roosevelt embarked last March is not a new one in history; it was only the drama of its immediate and critical environment which gave it special emphasis and color. He sought, with a passionate suddenness, to do, as it were overnight, something akin to what the Liberal Government in

England had sought to do after 1906. Like it, he had swept the country by an appeal to social justice. Like it, he seeks to discover the terms of a new social equation in which a crude and irrational economic process may be transformed into one which serves an acceptable social purpose. The aims of the Liberal Government foundered upon the antagonism of the possessing class; the latter, which refused terms to socialized liberalism, had, after the war, to confront a militant socialism impatient with their philosophy and its claims. Refusing the medicine of reform, they drifted into the position where they confronted, as its alternative, the surgery of revolution. And that is the alternative of universal history.

Is American experience to be different? Mr. Roosevelt, no doubt, has certain advantages on his side which were lacking to his English predecessors. He deals with a society far more experimental in character, far easier to shake out of its habitual ways. He has still a volume of popular support which no comparable foreign government has enjoyed. He still has the will and the courage to govern—assets which the Liberal Government of Great Britain lost far more easily than he is likely to do. He is dealing with a crisis; and a people in a crisis always responds to measures which have an imaginative sweep about them. He deals with a people ever more insistently aware that his failure is their own; more likely, accordingly, to realize the need on their part for patience in difficulty and ardor in support. He is attacking, further, a body of opponents whose own dismal failure to justify their leadership is made painfully more evident by every careful analysis of their past. He is appealing from irrationalism to principle, with the clear knowledge that, if he fails, irrationalism will again resume its empire over men's lives.

More than that, there is also the knowledge that, if he does fail, forces march to the conflict between whom decision is no longer possible in terms of peace. The failure of Mr. Roosevelt means the end of political democracy in America, for the simple reason that it will prove itself thereby incapable of adapting to its purposes the institutions of its economic life.

These are important advantages which we gain nothing by minimizing; yet they do not provide a basis for optimism. There is too little evidence in the American scene to suggest in the predominant economic forces any anxiety to coöperate in their radical adaptation. Wall Street may fairly be likened to the British House of Lords; and of the latter it was said acutely by Lord Rosebery that it would pass only in a storm. It is important that there is absent from America a trained and neutral civil service; this makes

Mr. Roosevelt's administrative problem one of grave magnitude. It is important, also, that the separation of powers surrounds the executive control of Congress with the constant hazard of uncertainty; to control it, he must be successful, and he lacks the assurance of success. Nor is the prospect of conflict with the Supreme Court a negligible factor; psychologically not uneager to wound, a decay in the resolution of public opinion might easily endow it with the courage to strike.

Behind all is the terrible factor of time, the need for rapid accomplishment, the danger that delay in success may split the forces upon whose unity the President depends for victory. And it is a factor of importance that he deals with a world situation in which, both economically and politically, reason seems to have lost its hold over men's minds and hearts.

What Mr. Roosevelt is doing is, in a general way, what any President must have sought to do who had achieved power on his terms; though it must be added that, in the conditions of presidential nomination, few would have sought to do it either with his courage or with his persistence. What he is doing is to find those intermediate terms between traditional America and that new American society the ultimate emergence of which is written in the inescapable facts of her economic and social life. He is seeking that commonwealth which those facts alone make rational—a commonwealth the values of which men feel able to accept as just because they *are* rational. If he fails, in the end, other men will take up his work, though it will be by very different methods that they will achieve his purpose. But if he succeeds, he will write a new page in the history of the world. For, having saved America by his energy, he will, as one trusts, save Europe by his supreme example.

14

A CRITIQUE OF NEW DEAL SOCIAL PLANNING AS IT AFFECTS NEGROES

Ralph J. Bunche *

In 1932 nearly three out of four Negro voters supported the Republican party; in 1936 three out of four voted for Franklin Roosevelt. This switch occurred even though New Deal programs often followed Jim Crow lines and even though Roosevelt, who considered civil rights less important than recovery, always insisted that racial discrimination could be eliminated only by a gradual process of education. The New Deal did, however, provide tangible benefits for the black population, particularly through federal relief: by 1935 thirty percent of Negroes were on welfare rolls, and the percentage was even higher in northern cities where the black vote was concentrated. Many New Dealers—among them Eleanor Roosevelt—openly favored integration, and several Negroes were appointed to government office; also, the President was not customarily held responsible for congressional failure to enact civil rights legislation. But if many Negroes viewed the New Deal with favor, many others—particularly intellectuals—bitterly criticized its inadequacies. Few offered more devastating attacks than did Ralph Bunche, who was then teaching political science at Howard University. After the Second World War Dr. Bunche, who played a key role in the United Nations and won the Nobel Peace Prize, would come to be regarded as a moderate in the civil rights movement. But his analysis of the New Deal in 1936 stemmed from thoroughly radical assumptions, and it raised questions—about the capacity of the middle classes to bring about far-reaching reforms, the manner in which the New Deal heightened racial stereotypes and injustice, and the relationship between economic and racial reform—that call for serious consideration. Perhaps Bunche's most important contribution was to link the New Deal's impact upon the Negro with its effect upon American society as a whole. □

---

*Bunche, Ralph J., A Critique of New Deal Social Planning As It Affects Negroes, *Journal of Negro Education,* V (January, 1936), 59-65. Reprinted by permission of the *Journal of Negro Education.*

NEW DEAL "EQUILIBRIUM"

The New Deal, at its inception, confronting an economy of chaos, proclaimed its major purpose to be the application of planning to our entire social structure. In pursuance of this objective a whole series of complicated and contradictory mechanisms have been invented and set up with the purpose of effecting a regulated orderliness in the economic life of the nation. But after two years of frantic trial and error, the New Deal, and most of its elaborate machinery, remains suspended in mid-air, bewildered, and innocuous. Relief expenditures have continued to rise, and unemployment was greater at the end of the year 1934 than it was in December, 1933. Even the staunchest supporters of the New Deal, though still weakly professing optimism, are often compelled to admit that its ideology is illogical, inconsistent, vague, and confused; that its program is composed of a mass of self-contradictory experimentation, and that, in its unblushing rôle of political coquette, it turns now to the left, now to the right.

The explanations of the New Deal and of its apparent failure are not far to seek. The New Deal merely represents our domestic phase of the almost universal attempt in capitalistic countries to establish a new equilibrium in the social structure; an attempt made necessary by the fact that the collapse of the economic structures under the world-wide depression brought out, in bold relief, the sharp class antagonisms which the developing capitalistic economies had nurtured. The history of the operation of social forces in the Western world since the World War is sharply outlined in at least two particulars: (1) Capitalists, *ie.*, Big Owners, have clearly indicated their inability and unwillingness to afford any leadership in the society which would promise even a meager measure of social justice to the masses of population, though the productive and organizational genius of capitalism is unchallenged; (2) on the other hand, the working classes of the countries of Western Europe, Russia excepted, though winning their way to a position of real power in the state, completely failed to take over the controls of the state, either through political channels or by force. The result has been a significant upsurge of the middle classes of the Western world, whose claim to national leadership is predicated on their assumed ability to reconcile these conflicting class interests in the society through the establishment of a new equilibrium;–a new society, in fact, in which conflicting group interests and inequalities will be merged in a higher national purpose.

Unwittingly or not, President Roosevelt was responsive to these social forces when he sounded the key note of the New Deal in his radio address of May 7, 1933.

It is wholly wrong to call the measures that we have taken government control of farming, control of industry, and control of transportation. It is rather a partnership in profits, for profits would still go to the citizens, but rather a partnership in planning and a partnership to see that the plans are carried out.

The New Deal which was then visited upon us embraced no significant shift of ideas, traditions, or loyalties. In large degree it represented merely an effort to refurbish the old individualistic-capitalistic system and to entrust it again with the economic destinies and welfare of the American people. It recognized, of course, that the American economy had slowed down, and particularly that the forces within it were no longer in equilibrium—a rude awakening for our traditional class-consciousless society. The intellectual pilots of the New Deal would remedy this condition, though certainly not by revolution, nor even by fascist counter revolution, (not immediately, at any rate); but in the words of one author: "abhorring the thought of violence and having no conscious class interests of their own, [they] have refused to agree that the mechanism has run down. They will wind it up again and, having done that, will suspend in balance and for all time the existing class relations in American soceity."[1]

THE TENETS OF THE NEW DEAL

Certain postulates have been laid down as fundamental in the New Deal program. The private ownership of the means of production is to continue, but on the one hand, capitalism must be stopped from exploiting the producers of its raw materials and, on the other, its labor supply. Agriculture, despite its over-capitalized plant and its reluctant but almost complete restriction to the domestic market, is to be permitted a large enough return to allow for the meeting of fixed charges and the purchase of capital and consumer's goods. Wage-earners, although it is admitted that in a machine economy there are too many of them in the white-collar and laboring categories, are to be assured employment and at least the means of subsistence, with a large hope thrown in for incomes conducive to a decent standard of living.

Our own rather short experience with middle-class planning, not to

---

[1] Hacker, *Short History of the New Deal,* 26.

mention the clearer and even more disastrous experiences of Italy, Germany, and Austria with similar schemes, permits us to raise a serious question concerning the ability of the middle classes to construct a new equilibrium which will afford a proper consideration of the interests of the masses of the population. The weakness of the middle classes is precisely that they are "in the middle," *i.e.,* they hold an intermediate position between the working masses and the finance capitalists. Included in their ranks are many whose economic status is continually precarious, and who are weak, uncourageous, and unskillful. In the U.S. today they are largely petty bourgeois. There are many who would incline sympathetically toward the cause of the proletariat, but there are many others whose aspirations ally them ideologically with big business, thus adding greater confusion to the American scene.

Yet this rather ambiguous middle class,–opportunistic and ambitious, lacking class cohesion and ideology–whose members have been completely captivated by the lure of the American Dream, has but two alternatives in the present situation. The middle class itself must take over and operate industry or it must allow private industry to retain its tenacious grip on the economic structure of the nation. But the middle-class leadership is well aware of the violent nature of the struggle that would be necessary in any attempt to wrest industry out of the hands of big ownership. Consequently, the tendency is to take the easier path and to employ the power of the state to keep the masses in check while handling the industrialists with velvet gloves. That is merely another way of saying that the working masses become ever more dependent upon the intervention of the state in their struggle to obtain social justice from the owners and directors of industry. But coincidentally, the alliance between the middle-class political power and the economic power of big business, becomes more unholy. Italy and Nazi Germany afford classic illustrations of the sort of "balance" the working masses can expect from such a process.

The dilemma of the New Deal, then, merely reflects the basic dilemma of capitalism. Either capitalism must surrender itself to intelligent and scientific social planning, (and this it cannot do, for such planning involves a single ownership of the means of production for use rather than for profit), or else it must blunder on, repeating the errors and perpetuating the rigidities which inevitably lead a poorly planned industrial society into periodic depression.

The measures of intervention employed by the New Deal have really been measures of state capitalism which have already been employed by social democratic and fascist governments in Europe, and which obviously have not restored prosperity there, nor settled any of the fundamental conflicts within the modern capitalistic state.

Class lines are more sharply drawn, but state capitalism attempts to balance these class interests within the limits of middle-class democracy. The NRA, for example, began with sympathetic gestures toward labor, if section 7a can be so considered. But it soon became a means of preventing and settling strikes, usually to the disadvantage of labor, as witnessed by the defeat of labor in the settlements of the automobile, San Francisco, textile and other strikes.

American state capitalism has no choice but this, for it proposes to salvage the old order. It retains formal democracy and may make minor concessions to labor. The government intervenes to aid industry, to limit output. But this is not the planned economy of socialism, where all phases of economic activity are placed under planful regulation and control, because here class interests remain in bitter conflict and big ownership retains its economic power. It is not without great significance to the subject of middle-class planning under capitalism, that Secretary Wallace, in his book *New Frontiers,* readily acknowledges, with amazing frankness for one in his position, the enormous influence wielded over the New Deal administration and legislation by the paid lobbies of powerful industrial interests. He clearly suggests that several of the important features of the New Deal represent, not the mature wishes and policies of the Roosevelt administration, but the demands of self-seeking pressure groups, whose demands were too insistent and vigorous to be withstood. The NRA and its codes, he confesses, were not the brain-children of the brain-trusters, but were the products of a swarm of hard-headed business men intent on group price-fixing, who swooped down on Washington and its New Dealers. In America, then, the New Deal follows the classical pattern of middle-class planning by compromise with Big Business,—a policy fatal to the interests of labor.

THE NEW DEAL AND THE NEGRO

For the Negro population, the New Deal means the same thing, but more of it. Striking at no fundamental social conditions, the New Deal at best can only fix the disadvantages, the differentials, the discriminations, under which the Negro population has labored all along. The traditional racial stereotypes,–which have been inherited from the master-slave tradition and which have been employed by the ruling class of large land-holders in the South and industrialists in the North to give effective expression to their determination to keep the Negro in a servile condition and as a profitable labor supply,–remain, and are indeed, often heightened by the New Deal.

Intelligent analysis and the dictates of a purely selfish policy of promoting the profit motive should have made clear to the NRA that the competitive exploitation of any significant part of the population, such as the Negro, would frustrate its efforts toward recovery. The poverty of the Negro is an ever-present obstacle to the prosperity of the dominant population. Therefore the first efforts of the NRA should have been directed toward assuring Negro workers that real wage which would make possible for them a decent standard of living.

Negro Wage Earners

To the contrary, however, from the beginning, relatively few Negro workers were even theoretically affected by the labor provisions of NRA. The evils of part-time work, irregular work and occupational and wage differentials, suffered especially by the great mass of Negro workers in the South, were perpetuated under NRA. Through the codes, occupational and geographical differentials were early used as a means of excluding Negro workers from the benefits of minimum wage and hour provisions. Subsequently, the continuation of the inferior economic status of the Negro was assured by NRA through code provisions basing wage rates on the habitual wage differential existing between Negro and white workers. Such measures failing to keep Negro wages at the desired low level, there was still the device of securing a specific exemption from the code of the Negro wage-earners in any given plant. In the power laundry code approved by the President, in an industry employing nearly 30,000 Negro women, a 14 cent per hour minimum wage was established, and even this miserable level was not enforced. Dr. Peck,[2] Executive Director of the Labor Advisory Board, who has maintained staunchly that the NRA has benefited Negro workers, in that the "rates in codes have greatly narrowed the differentials which existed before codes," admits however, that in the service industries in which so many Negroes are employed, "habit, standard of living, cost of living and the level of income of the local population may have a long-time result in a continuance of differential

---

[2]The Negro Worker and the NRA, *Crisis,* S 1934.

wages." To make still more illusory the theoretical benefits of the NRA to Negro wage-earners, the compliance machinery has been so constructed and operated as virtually to deny any just treatment to the Negro workman, especially in the South.

The FERA relief figures portray graphically enough the effect of NRA upon the Negro. In October, 1933, approximately 2,117,000 Negroes were in families registered on relief rolls, or about 18 per cent of the total Negro population in 1930. In January, 1935, about 3,500,000 Negroes in families on relief were reported, approximating 29 per cent of the 1930 population. Most significantly, too, the proportion of Negroes on relief in relation to total population was greater in rural than in urban centers. In addition, it is reliably estimated that there are now some 1,000,000 male Negroes unemployed, exclusive of agricultural pursuits.

Agriculture

The dilemma of American Agriculture is the dilemma of the American economy. There are too many farmers and too much land in cultivation, just as there are too many industrial workers and too much industrial production. These surpluses exist because American agriculture and industry have developed too much efficiency for our profit-motivated economic system. The welfare of the Negro farmer is bound up in the government's solution to the basic dilemma of capitalism—the necessity of providing a decent standard of living, based on a much higher consumption level, for all of the surplus workers and farmers, while retaining an economic order which is founded on profit and not on use. The New Deal, in its agricultural program expressed through the AAA, grabbed vigorously at one horn of the dilemma, and the Negro farmer and farm worker have been left dangling precariously from the other. It goes without saying that the Negro tenant farmer has borne more than his share of this burden. The AAA bears the responsibility for other methods of fixing the Negro population as a poverty-stricken group. It has winked at wide-spread violations of the rights of tenant farmers under the crop-reduction contracts; though the acreage reductions under the government rental agreements dispensed with the need of a great number of the tenants, the government contract theoretically proscribed the reduction of tenants by the land owner. The AAA has blandly permitted the white owner to employ the traditional methods of intimidation of the Negro to deprive him of his benefits from the crop reduction program in payment of parity checks.

The apparent failure of the government's pay-as-you-*not*-grow agricultural program, the growing conviction that the European market for our agricultural products is gone for good, together with the ever-present worry of too many farmers and too much land—we could probably get along with about one-half the number of farmers we now have and could remove from cultivation one-third to one-half of the land now used through the application of efficiency and technical advances to the industry. It is these conditions which have compelled the administration in desperation to flirt with the essentially fantastic "planning" scheme of subsistence homesteads. This scheme proposes to move the inefficient farmers, who thereby are doomed, out of their present economic graveyards and transplant them to semi-rural villages, where they will establish "model" communities. Living on plots ranging from five to forty acres, they will continue to till the soil, but only for family consumption, and are supposed to undergo a sort of economic atavism by reviving the fine old peasant pastimes of pottery making, woodwork, spinning, weaving, etc. To keep life from becoming too monotonous, as it most certainly would under such positive economic security, the government will provide some "factory" seeds for them to plant in the early spring. After the transplanted farmers get through fiddling around in their garden plots, and have indulged in a bit of handicraft, they will thus have the chance to pick up a bit of pin money for automobiles, radios and electric refrigerators, by working in the factories. In this way the submarginal farmer is to be kept on the land and so prevented from swelling the steadily mounting ranks of the industrial unemployed, and likewise kept out of competitive production. In other words the subsistence homesteader will be lifted out of the mainstream of our economic life and laid up on an economic shelf to dry (rot).

The real catch to the scheme is of course in the fact that the bill for the construction, the equipment, repair, taxation, and provision of social services for these communities of "official" peasants, will be footed chiefly by the employed industrial wage earners and the producing commercial farmers; not to mention the serious consequences for a capitalism which thrives on markets and profits, resulting from the consequential contraction of its domestic market for both consumer's and capital goods. This policy Mr. Webster Powell and Mr. Harold M. Ware aptly call "planning for permanent poverty."

Insofar as the program has applied to Negroes it has followed the traditional patterns of racial discrimination and segregation, two Jim Crow projects for Negroes having been recently established.

Primarily, the New Deal is a great relief program which guarantees at level best only a precarious livelihood of the most meager essentials for the millions of distressed workers and farmers who are on the outside of our economic life looking in. Middle-class New Deal planning has adequately demonstrated an utter inability to attain its necessary objectives of lower prices, greater output, and elimination of unemployment in industry. The New Deal policy of planning by separate private industries inevitably tends to raise prices and restrict output,–that is to say, it tends to perpetuate an economy of scarcity. Whether consciously or not, it has placed agricultural scarcity in competition with industrial scarcity, and the resultant increases in the prices of both agricultural and manufactured products have deepened the economic depression in which both agriculture and industry had sunk. It has shown only confusion when faced with the problem of administering prices and production in the interest of the whole population.

In the nature of the case it could at best do but little for the Negro within the existing social structure. The Negro does not even boast a significant middle class which, at least, might share some of the gains made for that class by the New Deal. For the Negro middle class exists, in the main, only psychologically, and can be briefly defined as "a hope, a wish and caricature." In fact, the New Deal planning only serves to crystallize those abuses and oppressions which the exploited Negro citizenry of America have long suffered under laissez-faire capitalism, and for the same reasons as in the past.

15
THE PRESIDENT'S POLITICAL STRATEGY
Walter Millis*

As a vital reform movement, the New Deal lasted only five years. Nearly every major reform that is today linked with the New Deal—social security, the TVA, the Wagner Act—had been enacted by 1935, and those passed somewhat later—public housing, wages and hours legislation—were on the books by 1938. Midway through his second term, in the belief that further reform required the liberalization of his party, Roosevelt embarked upon an effort to rid it of conservatives, to relieve it of those, he said, who did not deep in their hearts believe in New Deal principles. Yet his effort to purge the party succeeded only in New York City where John O'Connor, Chairman of the House Rules Committee, went down to a narrow primary defeat at the hands of a Roosevelt backer. In the South, where the need for it was greatest, the purge met with a sorry defeat. Senators Walter George of Georgia, Millard Tydings of Maryland, "Cotton Ed" Smith of South Carolina, and others easily won reelection; thus, even before the Republican victory in the congressional elections, it was clear that the New Deal was in deep trouble. It is against this background that Walter Millis' essay should be read. Millis, who was an editorial writer for the New York *Herald Tribune,* had written books on American entry into the Spanish-American War (*The Martial Spirit*) and World War I (*Road to War.*) In the autumn of 1938 he offered a shrewd evaluation of what the New Deal had done and why it had ground to a halt. □

Considering the passionately embittered controversy which daily rages around the New Deal, considering the great numbers to whom it is a vivid embodiment of hope and the other great numbers to whom it is the living figure of every evil principle in our public life, it is remarkable how few have noticed that the New Deal itself has passed into a purely historical importance. Yet this would seem to be the clearest fact emerging from the chaos of our contemporary scene. The controversial artillery is thundering

---

*Millis, Walter, The President's Political Strategy, *The Yale Review,* XXVIII (September, 1938), 1-10, 18.

over an abstraction which is really of very slight contemporary significance; the furious war is being waged around a phantom of past policies, past hates and enthusiasms and fears, now largely committed to history. To-day there is no New Deal. There are still New (and Old) Dealers; there is a hodgepodge of often conflicting policies and politicians set in a very uncertain economic context; there are idealists and coattail riders, earnest theoreticians and ambitious practical men—and there is always the President. But the New Deal of 1933 is now so completely enshrined in the past that even its bitterest opponents find it very difficult to explain precisely what it is that they are to-day opposing, and its strongest supporters—if the course of the summer primaries is any indication—seem too confused or indifferent to be capable of supporting it.

"I should like to have it said of my first Administration," the President exclaimed in the triumphant closing hours of his campaign of two years ago, "that in it the forces of selfishness and lust for power met their match. I should like to have it said of my second Administration that in it these forces met their master." But it has not worked out that way. Setting out to translate his spectacular victory into action, he was defeated on the Supreme Court bill, defeated on reorganization, got only an attenuated version of the wage-hour bill enacted, with difficulty stemmed a congressional rebellion seeking to snatch the spending power from his hands, and stumbled into a severe economic collapse. It is not too much to say that now—two years after the people overwhelmingly "approved," as he said, "the policies and goal of the New Deal"—the New Deal itself has been reduced to a movement with no program, with no effective political organization, with no vast popular party strength behind it, and with no candidate. It is further embarrassed, paradoxically enough, by the fact that it is without even an opposition.

There is no longer a New Deal program. This is partly because the President's policies have failed in some respects; it is mainly because they have worked too well. He is the victim of his own success. The New Deal was born of the extreme crisis of 1933. Whether the President's energetic intervention in that emergency (acclaimed at the time by nearly all classes and all sections) saved an economic system on the brink of self-destruction or irretrievably debauched it in the moment when it was just struggling back to sanity will no doubt be long debated, and is now quite irrelevant. In snatching up what seemed only the simpler and more obvious remedies, the President actually succeeded in transforming that system profoundly, and it is now a new time, new issues, and new conditions which confront us. What will probably be regarded as the New Deal's essential contribution to American history has already been made, not only beyond any reasonable probability of its undoing but also, unhappily for the President, beyond possibility of repetition.

Mr. Roosevelt instituted a system of emergency agricultural relief, and thereby finally established the principle—for which agrarian rebellion had been contending since the days of the greenbackers—of permanent federal subsidy to agriculture comparable to the tariff subsidies and financial advantages so long enjoyed by industry. He flung a few hundred millions into the maw of the unemployment crisis, and succeeded in committing the nation to an almost certainly permanent system of federal unemployment relief and subsidized "security," with all the complicated effects upon wage levels, labor supply, and political controls which inevitably go with it. He destroyed the gold standard, set out to instil probity into the stock exchanges and responsibility and decorum into the processes of company promotion; these measures, in conjunction with the banking legislation and the huge deficits consequent upon the other aspects of his program, resulted in the transfer to the federal government of a very large share of the control over the vital financial mechanism which had previously been left to the unregulated hand of private enterprise. And finally, with this extension of government into the sacred business of organizing the capital resources of the country, he coupled a more confused but no less significant entry into the business of organizing its labor supply. The wage-hour bill is one aspect of this effort; the Wagner Act another one. For the first time, the force of federal law was placed behind the union organizer, and government was dedicated to the inordinately difficult task of regulating and promoting the concentration of human, no less than of economic, power which modern industry necessitates.

These were the essential contributions of the New Deal. Other things were incidentals—often important in themselves, but incidentals which may or may not survive. It is safe to say that a subsidized agriculture, a subsidized relief and "security" system, a managed currency and managed exchanges will remain. In principle, none of these contributions was seriously contested by the Republicans in 1936, and Governor Landon has recently enunciated what will doubtless become his party's general policy towards them—accepting these revolutionary changes effected by the Democrats, it is now the mission of the Republicans "to make them work." While Dr. Frank's policy committee, announcing that "we have made genuine headway in defining and accepting our social obligation to young and old," seem in effect to echo him. The future of the Wagner Act is perhaps less certain, but even if it should be seriously modified, it is unlikely that the underlying principle of federal regulation of labor relations will be abandoned.

The New Deal has been dealt. That cannot be done over again. It has given the nation a far more compact political and economic system than the still relatively loose structure which existed in 1932; it has concentrated a vastly greater measure of power in Washington and particularly in the presidency, thereby making the struggle for the control of that power far more important, more desperate, and more bitter; while in giving numerically large blocs of the electorate a direct stake in the favors of government, it has by-passed the old political, financial, and industrial leaders among whom those favors were once regularly parcelled out for subsequent distribution to the masses, thus upsetting many of the comfortable old forms in which that struggle was carried on. These are considerable achievements. They do not conceal the fact that the New Deal has failed to produce that secure and balanced economy, functioning with an even prosperity and dispensing a nicely-proportioned "social justice" to all the several great classes and interests, which the President expected from it. In the face of the 1937 depression, of the furious hatreds and confusions in the field of labor relations, of the overhanging deficit and the continued refusal of private capital to return to work, it is unnecessary to emphasize the fact that while a new situation has been established, the problem of what is to be done with it is almost as urgent as ever. The New Deal has been dealt; the President (not to speak of the country) finds himself still faced with the intricate and embarrassing question of how the cards are to be played under the new conditions which it has created. If he has worked out a new program for this vital stage of the game, the public is unaware of it. So far, he seems scarcely even to have begun the bidding.

Without a program, the New Deal is likewise without a party. Here is to be noted one of the most embarrassing of its omissions, only now becoming fully apparent. Amid all the revolutionary changes over which he has presided, the President never constructed for himself either the organized party machinery or the convinced popular following through which to make any consistent new program effective. The New Deal has left him with enormous political assets. The New Dealers have Mr. Hopkins's estimated ninety per cent of the relief vote; they have great numbers of the subsidized small farmers; they have an important following of organized labor and retain great strength scattered through the lower middle classes, especially in those poorer sections of the South or West where the whole social structure, from top to bottom, has most directly felt the revivifying influence of the New Deal billions. And they have the still powerful personal popularity of Mr. Roosevelt, founded upon the direct benefits which all these groups have received. But one has only to contrast the personal triumph of the President's journey through the West in July with the spotty, aimless, and, on the whole, adverse results of the primaries, to perceive how badly most of these assets have been frozen.

Up until the time of the President's return from his ocean cruise, the results everywhere seemed to be tending towards the same general conclusion. In Pennsylvania the party was captured by theoretical New Dealers, but in circumstances which made the victory far worse than a defeat. Challenges to the old-line Democratic machines in Iowa and Virginia were easily defeated; in Indiana, in Missouri, in Colorado, and in Nevada the challenge was not even made. In Texas no clear issue could be drawn; the voters wandered aimlessly among the various candidates with erratic results, which were, however, well calculated to bring aid and comfort to the conservative forces of "Cactus Jack" Garner. Idaho was lost to an avowed opponent of the President. In Kentucky the President saved his Senate majority leader; the success was tactically important for the coming battles in Congress, but the New Deal was not at issue and the outcome had little significance for matters of basic principle.

The New Deal victories in Florida, Oklahoma, and Ohio were not much to set against all this. Generally speaking, the strategy of the "elimination committee" was in ruins; indeed, it had apparently been tacitly abandoned by the President before his oratorical special was fairly under way. "The politics of principle," launched by the small group of brilliant theoreticians who are almost the only true centre of New Deal strength remaining, was proving to be all principle and no politics; for the votes were not in it. And even the "inevitable historical process," relied upon by those who noted to how great an extent the power of the purse and patronage had been transferred from the state machines to the national capital, seemed somehow not to be proceeding.

For there were fatal defects in it. In the absence of a genuine New Deal national machine, it was still largely through the local organizations that the pap had to be distributed; they remained the obstinate (and often, as in Pennsylvania, the malodorous) bottlenecks through which the federal influence still had to pass. While the power of the purse, in a more fundamental sense, is a power which, once exercised, tends to lose its potency. So firmly did the New Deal establish the idea of a subsidized agriculture, and a subsidized relief system and wage structure, that the populace has come to take it for granted. These huge new forms of federal aid may continue to contribute to the President's personal popularity, but until there appears some really organized, explicit, and determined assault upon them (and none, certainly, has appeared so far) they are unlikely to be of much service as the energizing principles of an effective presidential party.

No longer seriously concerned about the continuation of the bounties, the electorate has been free to quarrel with the mode of their distribution, as many of the Western farmers are now doing; to wander off, with the Texas voters, after the novelties of radio advertising and the illusory attractions of new pension schemes; to become entangled, as in Kentucky, with the futilities of an empty factionalism; or to fall back into the traditional arms of such old-fashioned political machines as that of Mayor Hague in Jersey City or the San Antonio organization, which retired Mr. Maury Maverick, the ablest, most vigorous, and most honest New Dealer in Congress. And while all sorts of different economic and sectional blocs may share a common enthusiasm for the President, it has not prevented them from fighting among themselves with a bitterness which has everywhere checked the President's effort to combine them into a single, consistently co-ordinated political force.

When he placed the power of the federal government behind union organization, Mr. Roosevelt did not get in return the united support of organized labor, but only the paralyzing struggle between the A.F. of L. and the C.I.O. This was quickly compounded by the small shopkeeper and middle-class conservative's fear of C.I.O. "communism," by the agrarian distrust of the urban proletariat and the South's resentment of Northern industrial power. Relief not only involves its scandals but its jealousies; the more ignorant Southern white worker can point bitterly at the "nigger-lover" in the White House who has put Negroes on W.P.A. and assisted Negro tenant farmers, and the catalogue could be indefinitely extended. The field is open for the exploitation within the pro-Roosevelt voting masses of every crudity, every emotional appeal or economic conflict, which the ingenuity of the ambitious professional politician or calculating conservative may suggest; and these primaries seemed clearly enough to demonstrate the futility and aimlessness to which the vast pro-Roosevelt electorate has in this way been reduced.

Virtually nowhere, I believe, save in Idaho did any important

Democratic candidate fail to declare himself a devoted Roosevelt man in sympathy with the general purposes of the New Deal; yet nearly everywhere the victory was tending to go to those to whom the frankly anti-New Dealers were giving their support. In several of the strongly Democratic States where a destined victim of the disciplinary "purge" was running, one was told that his success would in no way imply that popular defeat for the New Deal which the Republican and anti-Roosevelt press was prepared to see in it. No doubt, in one sense this was true. In returning the old-line politicians, whose deviations from the true doctrine were often subtle, well-concealed, and unconfessed, the populace was probably not, in most cases, intending to vote against the President or against the vague general concept to which the New Deal has now been reduced. But the defeat was no less serious. For the result showed that the pro-Roosevelt electorate, between its own divisions over specific elements in the President's policies and its involvement with the traditional local machines, was incapable of making its enthusiasm practically effective. The President had an army but no cause; he may have vast numbers of the voters, but he was without a party.

Such was the state of affairs, and such were the obvious conclusions upon which the President had plenty of time to reflect as his cruiser steamed homeward through the Caribbean. The result of the reflections was apparent as he reached the soil of Georgia. The strategy of the "elimination committee," quietly laid aside on the road to the Southwest, was suddenly revived. There came the dramatic attack upon Senator George, in which the President drew the issue between "a liberal on the one side and a dyed-in-the-wool conservative on the other" more sharply than he had ever done before, and laid down "a constant, active, fighting attitude in favor of the broad objectives of the party and the government *as they are constituted to-day*" as the clear test to be applied by Democratic voters. There came the short but sharp rap at Senator Smith in South Carolina—which did not prevent him from winning out. There came the lightning bolt hurled suddenly from a presidential press conference against Senator Tydings in Maryland and Representative O'Connor in New York. Characteristically enough, the President's reaction was to put up a fight—when it was all but too late.

One can only await the consequences. No doubt, a New Deal victory in all these contests would have altered the psychology of the situation. Yet it could not have removed the considerable number of old-line

Democrats and anti-New Dealers already assured of seats in the coming Congress, while to most observers the chances of victory in any of the remaining primaries seem pretty slim. They seem so slim, indeed, as to suggest that the last-minute presidential belligerence is designed more for the moral than for the practical effect. Though it fails to unseat Senator George and the others, it may still lay the basis for a popular campaign around which the electorate may be rallied next year into a true presidential party. Perhaps—but one is inclined to doubt it; and without a popular party it will now be extremely difficult for the President to weld the variegated hosts of politicians, administrators, theoreticians, and very practical men who have ridden into power on his victories into an even reasonably cohesive and disciplined governmental machine.

It was because of this failure to create a genuine popular party that the unparalleled triumph of 1936 led only to the chaos and disappointments of 1937; it is for this reason that the confusions of 1938 now point to an even harder road through 1939 and 1940. The President's own fondness for the middle-of-the-road, his useful belief in "co-operation," his very skill at achieving his effects by the combination of opposites—a Farley with a Hopkins, a La Follette with a Lewis, a Corcoran with a Hague—were always a constant invitation to private insurgency. The general course of the primaries now seems to put a premium on it, for they apparently prove that its dangers were overrated. The President has lost his power to punish; and with that gone, a quietly decorous insurgency offers many easy, practical rewards. It means that a President who lives by action finds the platform of organization support in Congress, from which any vigorous and dramatic new action must be launched, now shaking and insecure beneath his feet. . . .

As to larger affairs, in the meanwhile, both the party and the nation will probably continue to roll and slat and plunge in these politcal doldrums watching the sails being trimmed from day to day to catch the fitful breezes of factional calculation while waiting for some new, strong wind of basic policy to spring up. This, it may be said, is a disappointing conclusion. Of what help will this be amid the pressing social and economic problems to which the times, not to mention the New Deal, have brought us; what light does this throw upon the dark realities of the immediate future? None, to be sure; but whoever supposed that such matters were a primary concern of the play of politics? The New Deal is over. To guess who is to control the vast powers of the new state it has created; to estimate how the capacities of that state are to be used, in whose interest and with what result; to depict the social and economic future which will be erected upon them, one must turn to some more fundamental study than that of political strategy.

BIBLIOGRAPHICAL ESSAY

This essay does not propose to list every book written about the New Deal; its purpose is to indicate some of the more important lines of inquiry pursued by historians in the last few years. I have omitted books published before 1963 which may be found in bibliographies in the standard works on the New Deal: Frank Freidel, *Franklin D. Roosevelt* (3 vols., Boston, 1952-1956); James M. Burns, *Roosevelt: The Lion and the Fox* (New York, 1956); Rexford G. Tugwell, *The Democratic Roosevelt* (New York, 1957); Arthur M. Schlesinger, Jr., *The Age of Roosevelt* (3 vols., Boston, 1957-1960); and William E. Leuchtenburg, *Franklin D. Roosevelt and the New Deal* (New York, 1963). Two other useful bibliographical aids are: William J. Stewart, *The Era of Franklin D. Roosevelt: A Selected Bibliography of Periodical and Dissertation Literature, 1945-1966* (Hyde Park, N.Y., 1967), and Richard S. Kirkendall, "The New Deal as Watershed: The Recent Literature," *Journal of American History,* **LIV** (March, 1968).

For many years after Roosevelt's death the questions most frequently asked of the New Deal were: How closely did it resemble earlier reform movements? How "revolutionary" was it? How much ideological consistency did it exhibit? That these questions remain of interest is evident in such works as that of Otis Graham, *An Encore for Reform: The Old Progressives and the New Deal* (New York, 1967). Graham found that a majority of progressives who lived on into the 1930's considered the New Deal too radical. Those who backed the new reform movement were likely to be from large cities and involved in welfare activities. Graham concludes: "To accept what Roosevelt and the New Dealers had done and wished to do demanded more openness to experiment with political institutions, more trust in the tractability of the state to democratic purposes, more willingness to turn the cumulated rancor of the lower third against the upper than most progressives could produce."

Most recent accounts of the 1930's, however, concentrate on the New Dealers themselves, the agencies and programs they fathered, the political coalition they built, and the challenges they encountered from both radicals and conservatives. Some of these studies take up at least indirectly the themes of continuity, radicalism and consistency. For example, Ellis Hawley has analyzed the National Recovery Administration in the broad context of public attitudes toward concentration and competition in *The New Deal and the Problem of Monopoly: A Study in Economic Ambivalence* (Princeton, N.J., 1966). His theme is that Americans wished to enjoy the benefits of large-scale business organization and yet retain older individualistic values. In general, early New Deal recovery agencies and the policies they followed have received an increasing amount of attention. The operation of the NRA in a particular industry is the subject of Sidney Fine's *The Automobile under the Blue Eagle: Labor, Management and the Automobile Manufacturing Code* (Ann Arbor, 1963). Efforts to regulate the stock market are discussed by Ralph F. DeBedt in *The New Deal's SEC: The Formative Years* (New York, 1964).

The Roosevelt administration's agricultural policies also have been explored in some detail. The impact of the Agricultural Adjustment Administration upon landless farmers is evaluated in David E. Conrad's *The Forgotten Farmers: The Story of Sharecroppers in the New Deal* (Urbana, 1965). John L. Shover, in *Cornbelt Rebellion: The Farmer's Holiday Association* (Urbana, Ill., 1965), investigates the social basis of one radical farm group and its influence upon Congress. New Deal efforts to aid marginal farmers later in the decade are evaluated by Louis Cantor in *A Prologue to the Protest Movement: The Missouri Sharecropper Roadside Demonstrations of 1939* (Durham, N.C., 1969), and Sidney Baldwin in *Poverty and Politics: The Rise and Decline of the Farm Security Administration* (Chapel Hill, N.C., 1967). Baldwin describes the various accomplishments of the agency but holds that "in a real sense the FSA represented a conservative or even reactionary attempt to sustain or restore a very unsatisfactory *status quo.*" In *Negroes and the Great Depression* (Westport, Conn., 1970), Raymond Wolters considers the impact of New Deal policies upon black Americans.

The creation of federal relief programs marked an important step in the development of the welfare state. Roy Lubove, in *The Struggle for Social Security, 1900-1935* (Cambridge, 1968), traces the origins of the old-age pension system, and Arthur J. Altmeyer's *The Formative Years of Social Security* (Madison, 1966) describes how the system functioned. One of the most popular relief ventures is explored by John A. Salmond in *The Civilian Conservation Corps, 1933-1942* (Durham, N.C., 1967). Some of the problems that occur when relief is combined with support for the arts are considered by Jane D. Mathews in *The Federal Theatre, 1935-1939: Plays, Relief and Politics* (Princeton, N.J., 1967), and William F. McDonald in *Federal Relief Administration and the Arts: The Origins and Administrative History of the Arts Projects of the Works Progress Administration* (Columbus, Ohio, 1969).

Franklin Roosevelt had great success in filling administrative posts with able and energetic men who have quite naturally attracted the interest of biographers. Searle F. Charles discusses the man most closely identified with welfare programs in *Minister of Relief: Harry Hopkins and the Depression* (Syracuse, N.Y., 1963). One phase of Henry Wallace's career is treated by Edward L. and Frederick H. Schapsmeier in *Henry A. Wallace of Iowa: The Agrarian Years, 1910-1940* (Ames, Iowa, 1969). The contributions to reform of an important brains truster are analyzed in Bernard Sternsher's *Rexford Tugwell and the New Deal* (New Brunswick, N.J., 1964). In *Senator Robert F. Wagner and the Rise of Urban Liberalism* (New York, 1968), J. Joseph Huthmacher examines the New York liberal who helped shape labor policy in the 1930's. The diaries of two New Deal officials have recently been published: John M. Blum, *From the Morgenthau Diaries* (3 vols., Boston, 1959-1967), and David E. Lilienthal, *The Journals of David E. Lilienthal: The TVA Years* (New York, 1964).

While Roosevelt was not the first President to draw advisors from the academic community, he did give scholars a large voice in the formulation of public policy. The role of social scientists in the development of the New Deal receives attention by Barry Dean Karl in *Executive Reorganization and Reform in the New Deal: The Genesis of Administrative Management, 1900-1939* (Cambridge, 1963), and Richard S. Kirkendall in *Social Scientists and Farm Politics in the Age of Roosevelt* (Columbia, Mo., 1966). Rexford G. Tugwell, in *The Brains Trust* (New York, 1968), and Raymond Moley, in *The First New Deal* (New York, 1966), offer quite different perspectives on Roosevelt's advisors. Tugwell's memoir provides a classic account of how Roosevelt's sense of the politically possible diluted broad-gauged proposals for economic reform.

Radicalism during the 1930's took a variety of forms, a few of which have been studied in depth. Father Coughlin and the Union Party of 1936 are considered in Charles Tull's *Father Coughlin and the New Deal*

(Syracuse, N.Y., 1965), David J. O'Brien's *American Catholics and Social Reform: The New Deal Years* (New York, 1968), David H. Bennett's *Demagogues in the Depression: American Radicals and the Union Party, 1932-1936* (New Brunswick, N.J., 1969), and Edward C. Blackorby's *Prairie Rebel: The Public Life of William Lemke* (Lincoln, Neb., 1963). Coughlin's sometime ally, Dr. Francis E. Townsend, is the subject of Abraham Holtzman in *The Townsend Movement: A Political Study* (New York, 1963). See also Jackson K. Putnam, *Old-Age Politics in California* (Stanford, Calif., 1970.) T. Harry Williams, in *Huey Long* (New York, 1969), offers a wealth of information on the conditions that produced—and the tactics employed by—one of the most feared men of the decade.

The appeal of radicalism to some intellectuals can be studied in James B. Gilbert's *Writers and Partisans: A History of Literary Radicalism in America* (New York, 1968), Frank A. Warren's *Liberals and Communism: The 'Red Decade' Revisited* (Bloomington, Ind., 1966), and Matthew Josephson's *Infidel in the Temple: A Memoir of the Nineteen-Thirties* (New York, 1967). Some of the bases of pacifist thought are explored by John K. Nelson in *The Peace Prophets: American Pacifist Thought, 1919-1941* (Chapel Hill, N.C., 1967). Dan T. Carter deals with the case that became a *cause célèbre* during the 1930's in *Scottsboro: A Tragedy of the Modern South* (Baton Rouge, 1969). Although radical thought during the depression focused almost exclusively on the revolutionary potential of the working class, workers' demands usually had little to do with socialism. For details in this area see Irving Bernstein, *Turbulent Years* (Boston, 1970) and Sidney Fine, *Sit-Down: The General Motors Strike of 1936-1937* (Ann Arbor, 1969).

As Earl Latham has demonstrated in *The Communist Controversy in Washington from the New Deal to McCarthy* (Cambridge, 1966), congressional investigating committees have often been employed by conservatives. During the 1930's, however, congressional inquiries served the purposes of liberals. The impact of the Nye Committee on attitudes toward the economic causes of war is considered by John E. Wiltz in *In Search of Peace: The Senate Munitions Inquiry, 1934-1936* (Baton Rouge, 1963). Jerold S. Auerbach's *Labor and Liberty: The LaFollette Committee and the New Deal* (Indianapolis, 1966) indicates how a congressional investigation could aid trade unions.

Conservative opposition to the New Deal, and the difficulties Roosevelt encountered after 1937, have aroused considerable interest. The role of rural Southern congressmen in frustrating liberal programs is

weighed by James T. Patterson in *Congressional Conservatism and the New Deal: The Growth of the Conservative Coalition in Congress, 1933-1939* (Lexington, Ky., 1967), Frank Freidel in *FDR and the South* (Baton Rouge, 1965), and John Robert Moore in *Senator Josiah William Bailey of North Carolina: A Political Biography* (Durham, N.C., 1968). Leonard Baker, *Back to Back: The Duel Between FDR and the Supreme Court* (New York, 1967), is useful; but more insight into the Court conflict is provided by Max Freedman (ed.) in *Roosevelt and Frankfurter: Their Correspondence, 1928-1945* (Boston, 1967), and in two essays by William E. Leuchtenburg: "The Origins of Franklin D. Roosevelt's 'Court-Packing' Plan," in Philip B. Kurland (ed.), *The Supreme Court Review* (Chicago, 1966), and "Franklin D. Roosevelt's Supreme Court 'Packing' Plan," in Harold M. Hollingsworth and William F. Holmes (eds.), *Essays on the New Deal* (Austin, Tex., 1969). The battle over administrative reform is considered in Richard Polenberg, *Reorganizing Roosevelt's Government: The Controversy over Executive Reorganization, 1936-1939* (Cambridge, 1966).

The role of the Republican Party in an era dominated by Democrats is explored by Donald McCoy in *Landon of Kansas* (Lincoln, Neb., 1966) and Ellsworth Barnard in *Wendell Willkie: Fighter for Freedom* (Marquette, Mich., 1966). The third term campaign of 1940 is the subject of several recent studies: Bernard F. Donohue, *Private Plans and Public Dangers: The Story of FDR's Third Nomination* (South Bend, Ind., 1965); Herbert S. Parmet and Marie B. Hecht, *Never Again: A President Runs for a Third Term* (New York, 1968); and Warren Moscow, *Roosevelt and Willkie* (Englewood Cliffs, N.J., 1968). V. O. Key, in *The Responsible Electorate: Rationality in Presidential Voting, 1936-1960* (Cambridge, 1966), analyzes the fate of the electoral coalition constructed by Franklin Roosevelt. A survey of the entire spectrum of anti-New Deal activity is provided by George Wolfskill and John A. Hudson in *All But the People: Franklin D. Roosevelt and His Critics, 1933-1939* (London, 1969).

While the social and intellectual history of the 1930's has received less attention than have economic and political developments, some attempts have been made to examine popular tastes and styles of thought in the decade. Three recent efforts are: Robert Bendiner, *Just Around the Corner: A Highly Selective History of the Thirties* (New York, 1967); Caroline Bird, *The Invisible Scar* (New York, 1966); and Louise Tanner, *All The Things We Were* (New York, 1968). Some aspects of music and the cinema are dealt with in Alan Lomax (ed.), *Hard Hitting Songs for*

Hard-Hit People: American Folk Songs of the Depression and the Labor Movement of the 1930's (New York, 1967), and Robert L. Snyder, *Pare Lorentz and the Documentary Film* (Norman, Okla., 1968). In *Ideologies and Utopias: The Impact of the New Deal on American Thought* (Chicago, 1969), Arthur A. Ekirch, Jr. attempts a synthesis of the intellectual history of the 1930's. He finds that the "nationalism or statism of the New Deal inaugurated the real revolution in modern American life and thought." See, in addition, Charles C. Alexander, *Nationalism in American Thought* (Chicago, 1969).

Concern about poverty, racism and war in the 1960's produced considerable criticism of American liberalism in general and of the New Deal in particular. Much of the "new left" indictment of the welfare state was, of course, voiced by the old left during the 1930's. Some of the issues involved in this critique are considered in: Barton J. Bernstein, "The New Deal: The Conservative Achievements of Liberal Reform," in Barton J. Bernstein (ed.), *Towards a New Past: Dissenting Essays in American History* (New York, 1968); Howard Zinn, "A Comparison of the Militant Left of the Thirties and Sixties," in Morton Frisch and Martin Diamond (eds.), *The Thirties: A Reconsideration in the Light of the American Political Tradition* (New York, 1968); and Jerold S. Auerbach, "New Deal, Old Deal, or Raw Deal: Some Thoughts on New Left Historiography," *Journal of Southern History,* **XXV** (February , 1969).